'The non-fiction book of the year'   Sarra Manning, *Red*

'This is not only an unflinching and powerfully told account of an unimaginably painful family tragedy. It is also an unforgettable meditation on a close sibling relationship, on growing up with grief, on life, love and everything in between. I am in awe of how Cathy has managed to write so bravely and beautifully'   *The Bookseller*

'A gobsmacking memoir about family and love. Truly, it will inspire you to be your very best self for a long time after the final page'   Alexandra Heminsley, *The Debrief*

'This is a touching and brave book, heartbreaking yet beautiful'   S. J. Watson, author of *Before I Go To Sleep*

'Incredibly powerful . . . The love that wraps itself around the pain and never goes away is what kept me turning the pages so quickly'   Rebecca Wait, author of *The View on the Way Down*

'Beautiful, devastating and ultimately uplifting, intimate and universal all at once . . . Cathy Rentzenbrink has found a way to express the things that all of us wrestle with at times – knowing how to live and taking the risk to love; facing what has damaged us, and owning it as much as a person can'   Jessie Burton, author of *The Miniaturist*

CATHY RENTZENBRINK

THE LAST ACT OF LOVE

The Story of My Brother and His Sister

PICADOR

First published 2015 by Picador

This paperback edition published 2016 by Picador
an imprint of Pan Macmillan
20 New Wharf Road, London N1 9RR
Associated companies throughout the world
www.panmacmillan.com

ISBN 978-1-4472-8639-4

1 3 5 7 9 8 6 4 2

A CIP catalogue record for this book is available from the British Library.

Printed and bound by CPI Group (UK) Ltd, Croydon, CR0 4YY

Visit www.picador.com to read more about all our books
and to buy them. You will also find features, author interviews and
news of any author events, and you can sign up for e-newsletters
so that you're always first to hear about our new releases.

For my original family:

my parents and my dear lost brother.

Oh, we ain't got a barrel of money
Maybe we're ragged and funny
But we'll travel along, singin' our song, side by side.

Harry Woods

Emergency brain surgery is very simple – it involves drilling holes in the skull and draining out blood – and is well within the competence of most junior doctors. The question of whether to operate to try to save the patient's life, however, is much more difficult.

Henry Marsh

THE PRAYER TREE

The chapel is not how I remember it. All these years I've imagined a simple wooden room buried deep in the hospital. Instead, light shines through a splendid stained-glass window onto an altar with an embroidered cloth and large brass candlesticks. It feels like a church.

I ask the chaplain if everything looks the same as it would have done when I was here over twenty years ago.

'We've had a new carpet,' she tells me, 'and pink covers for the seats. Though soot blows down from the roof so I'm always out here with a little hoover.'

There is a smallish tree to one side of the room with a blue-and-white cuddly elephant propped against the base and bits of coloured paper clipped among its leaves.

'That's newer,' the chaplain says. 'A prayer tree. That won't have been here when you were.'

I walk over to it and take one of the leaves between my thumb and forefinger. Plastic, but convincing from a distance. I read the messages written on the bits of paper. This must make it easier for atheists, I think. Far easier as an atheist *in extremis* to write something down and attach it to a tree than to kneel in front of an altar and try to work out how to make a deity you don't believe in listen to what you have to say. Some of the messages are addressed to God, some to the living, some to the dead. There is a range of handwriting styles, differing levels of ease with grammar and spelling. It is the badly punctuated ones that I find most poignant: I imagine they demanded the most effort. Some are in a spindly, elderly hand, others in childish rounded letters.

I hope the baby is alright when you have it.

15 years and I miss you like yesterday.

Dear God, thank you for listening.

Please pray for my little brother. Love you loads, little buddy.

For my dearest, greatly missed daughter. She died 25.10.83. I have never got over it.

Pray for us all.

I pause, lost in these hints and echoes of other people's stories, other people's love, and then wonder what I would have written if this tree had been in place when I stumbled in here on my way from intensive care to the relative's overnight room. I know what I wanted then, but how would I have found the words? To whom would I have addressed my plea?

Please don't let my brother die.
Dear God, please don't let my brother die.
Please pray for my brother. I don't want him to die.
Don't die, Matty, please don't die.

The years collapse, and I see myself kneeling and crying and begging, with my hands clasped together in prayer, talking to some unknown force.

Please don't let him die, please don't let him die, please, I'll do anything, only please don't let him die.

What strikes me now as it never has before is that I can't say my prayers went unanswered. I was given what I asked for. My brother did not die. But I did not know then that I was praying for the wrong thing. I did not know then that there is a world between the certainties of life and death, that it is not simply a case of one or the other, and that there are many and various fates worse than death. That is what separates the me standing here now by the prayer tree from the girl kneeling in front of the altar all those years ago. She thought she was living the worst night of her life, but I know now that far worse was to come. The thing she feared was that her brother would die, but I know now it would have been better for everyone if he had. It would have been better for everyone if, as she knelt here, begging for his life, his heart had ceased to beat, if the LED spikes on the monitors had turned into a flat line, if death had been pronounced, accepted, dealt with. It would have been so much better if Matty had died then.

She was praying for the wrong thing.

I was praying for the wrong thing.

THE EXISTENCE OF LOVE

We were spending a long, lazy, teenage Sunday afternoon in the garage at the back of the family pub. It was before the times of all-day opening, so the pub was shut and there were none of the usual comings and goings, no customers stopping to chat as they made their happy way home, no music from the jukebox floating out through the back door. It was just me, my younger brother Matty and our dog. Polly's parentage was unknown as she'd been thrown into the river in a sack when she was a puppy, but she looked like a black Labrador with a slightly curlier coat. She was never far from Matty's side, though she had to be tied up or the lure of the bins from the Chinese takeaway next door would prove too much. Her love for us was never proof against the temptation of discarded food.

The garage was huge, far from the one-car garage that we'd had in Almond Tree Avenue, the street in the next village we'd lived in until moving into the pub a year before. This beast could have fitted four or five cars and was an Aladdin's cave of oily delights. The previous owners hadn't cleared it out, so it was full of curious half-used tins with different-coloured drips down the sides. There were mechanical parts, old beer pumps, bits of lighting. It looked like anything broken in the pub had been slung in here in case a use could be found for it. There was an inspection pit, a big hole in the ground designed for people to get into so they could look underneath a car, Matty had some sort of science experiment going on that involved a vice, copper wire and beakers of liquid, and empty glasses were dotted around on the shelves and the floor. Recently Matty had got into big trouble with Mum and Dad for putting oil in a pint pot that ended up in the pub dishwasher and put it out of action, creating chaos on one of our busiest nights. Even Carol, the head barmaid, who adored him, had been unimpressed.

'He gets away with too much, that lad,' she'd said, shaking her head.

That afternoon, we were discussing the nature of love. Or rather, Matty was messing about with two broken-down motorbikes, taking parts off one to put on the other, and I was trying to get him to agree with me that love exists.

'I don't think so,' he said. 'It's an illusion. A trick to make people procreate and then look after their young.'

'But I know love exists because I feel it. Don't you?'

'I think love is a con. It's all about the continuation of the species.'

'Well, I love lots of people.'

Matty unscrewed a bolt. 'Who do you love?'

'Mum and Dad, obviously.' I reeled off a long list of relatives and friends.

'That's loads,' Matty said. 'And you really love them?'

'Yes, I do. And you. Maybe I even love you best of all.'

He grinned at me, oil smudged over his face. He had

5

considerable charm, my handsome brother: a fact of which he was well aware.

'Though I might take you off the list if there's no chance of being loved back.'

'Don't worry.' He picked up a rag and wiped his hands. 'I suppose if I love anyone then it's you. Is that good enough?'

'It'll do.'

A couple of weeks later, on another Sunday afternoon, we walked down to the riverbank to try out the salvaged motorbike on the dirt track there. Matty had succeeded in making one working machine out of the two wrecks and there was pride and pleasure in the way he wheeled it along. Occasionally he patted it. I was holding Polly's lead. I was not much interested in the bike but was happy to be tagging along; it was a beautiful day, all blue sky and picture-postcard clouds.

As soon as we got off the main road, I let Polly off the lead and she ran off to search for dead things to roll in. I stood and watched as Matty rode up and down the track. He looked enormous, entirely out of proportion. At sixteen he was only legally allowed to have a 50 cc motorbike, but he was six foot four so it looked too small for him. When he turned seventeen he would be able to upgrade to 125 cc, but my parents were trying to encourage him to get a car instead because they thought it would be safer.

Matty pulled up next to me, gravel chips flying.

'It's brilliant. Do you want to have a go? You can ride on the grass in case you fall off.'

It was an honour to be asked, though I hated the idea. I wasn't even that good at riding a pushbike. But I wanted to impress him and make him proud of me, so I agreed.

He gave me his gloves, far too big for me, and I straddled the bike, listened to all his instructions and jammed on the helmet. It smelt of oil and sweat and was a tight fit. I had a head like a fifty-bob cabbage, just like my dad, as one of our customers had recently delighted in telling me.

I set off. There was a brief period of exhilaration, a rush of air, a roar of joy. I wanted to shout out loud, 'I'm *riding a motorbike! I'm actually doing it!*' But then I forgot everything I was supposed to do. I wanted to slow down but the bike was going faster and faster and I didn't know how to make it stop. There was nothing else to do but part company: I pitched myself off to the side and tumbled onto the grass. The bike kept going, careering off in the other direction, before toppling over, while I lay on my back catching my breath and looking up at the fluffy white clouds. I didn't think anything hurt. Then Polly appeared and started snuffling around the visor, trying to get in to lick my face. Matty was kneeling over me.

'Are you all right?'

'I'm fine.' I sat up, feeling a bit dazed. He helped me pull off the helmet. I drank in the concern on his face.

'And you do love me,' I told him.

'What?'

'You ran to me rather than to your bike. I call that love.'

He laughed, 'You might be right. Don't get soppy about it, though.'

We collected the bike, no harm done, and walked home. A brother and sister with a motorbike and a dog.

Two weeks after that, I spent Sunday afternoon sitting next to Matty's unconscious body in an intensive care ward at Leeds General Infirmary. Whether or not he loved me had become irrelevant, but the fact that I loved him, probably best of all, meant that life was forever changed.

LAST ORDERS

I spent my last normal day as a teenager in Selby with my friend Chris. We lay on the grass under the trees in the little park near the bus station listening to Lou Reed on the cassette player that Chris always carried around with him. When 'Walk on the Wild Side' came on, Chris asked me what 'giving head' meant and I felt a bit superior that I knew and could tell him. Then we both hummed along to the opening chords of 'Perfect Day'. I looked up at the blue sky through the branches and leaves and felt certain that life was about to get way more exciting.

I had the words wrong. I thought Lou Reed was singing, 'You're going to reach, just watch yourself.' I thought he was promising me that great things lay ahead, but that I should make sure I looked after myself.

Chris had offered to paint a mural on my bedroom wall. It was currently a badly painted mess of green and purple because my parents had said 'decorate it how you like' when we'd moved in, and I'd chosen tins of sage and lilac paint from the DIY store in Selby but had lost interest after the first coat. I had the idea that I could get my friends to write poetry on the walls, but the first person to do it had misquoted Wordsworth and it looked a bit crap.

'I won't charge for my time,' Chris said, 'but I'll have to charge you for the paint, is that OK?'

I agreed. What a deliciously grown-up conversation, I thought. I tried it out in my head: I have an artist friend who will paint me a mural on my bedroom wall. I'll be paying for the paint.

We got the bus back to Snaith and I walked up through the village to the pub. I still had such a sense of pride that my parents owned the Bell and Crown and that I lived there, in a building that was mentioned in the parish records from 1633. The cellar was original, and I'd often go down there to listen for voices, making up plots for time-slip novels that featured barmaids through the ages.

Whenever I opened up, I would sit on a bar stool and read until the first customer arrived.

'Look at you with your nose in a book,' our customers would say. 'Book learning won't get you a husband.' They liked that I was good at the book clues in crosswords and on general knowledge shows, though.

And I liked talking to all the different types of people who came in. 'You're so sharp you'll cut yourself,' they'd say, and, 'What happened, did you swallow a dictionary?' But they taught me all sorts of things I didn't know, like how the names of racehorses were constructed and how to play dominoes for money. I learned how to say the Yorkshire-man's Motto in the right accent: ''Ear all, see all, say nowt. Eyt all, sup all, pay nowt; and if ivver tha' does owt for nowt, allus do it for thissen.' And 'Fuck 'em all, bar thee and me, and fuck thee, that's me.'

Matty was the delight of the ladies' darts team, who cooed and giggled over him: 'Ooh, I could get myself into trouble over that lad.'

'He's a cocky fucker, isn't he?' some man said to me over the bar.

'Maybe,' I said. 'He's got a good amount to be cocky about, to be fair.'

We were both enjoying the new authority and position we'd had since moving in the previous autumn. In our old village we were always viewed as outsiders, a bit odd and tricky to pin down. Dad was Irish, covered in tattoos, sang in the street and went to the pub a lot. If people liked Dad they called him a rough diamond, but not everybody did. Mum was a civil servant and hardly any women in our village went to work in a suit, so they made an especially odd pair. As for Matty and me, we were generally thought to be a bit too clever for our own good. Now, though, our eccentricity seemed to be playing in our favour. Everyone wanted to know us.

Life felt good. It hadn't always been easy for my dad being an Irishman in England, but by 1990 that had all changed and people loved the accent, the singing and the fact that he was extremely good *craic*. They called him Popeye or Forearms due to his enormous tattooed arms. 'You know she's Forearms' daughter?' said one man about me to another who was trying to chat me up. Some of our regulars had a game that involved thinking of combinations of things to buy that would come to £3.33 so they got to hear him say 'tree-tirty-tree'.

——

So now I had a bath and got ready for my shift behind the bar. I put on a cream shirt and a green suede jerkin I had bought from a charity shop, and orange three-quarter-length trousers that had blue-and-white-striped pockets. I tied some interwoven green and purple ribbons that I had first worn at a Wonder Stuff gig a couple of weeks before into my henna-red hair, and pulled on my doc shoes with no laces. I set off down the back stairs.

It was a usual Saturday night: busy, with people three or four deep at the bar. Matty and I each had our own section to serve and had got used to the art of it, which was way beyond pint-pulling. We had to make the people in our section feel confident that we knew what we were doing, that we knew their place in the jumbled-up queue.

'You're next,' we'd say, 'then you, then you,' shouting over the noise of the chat and the jukebox, pointing out the order so the customers felt reassured and wouldn't decide it was too busy here and go off to one of the other pubs in the village.

It was hard work – lots of running up and down the stone cellar steps to change barrels or fetch up more crates of bottled beer. We served and served, keeping an eye on the hands of the big clock as they edged towards ten to eleven.

We always squabbled over who got the treat of ringing the big brass bell for last orders, and that night, as every night, Matty won by the force of his height and his long arms, catching me and pinning me to his side with one arm as he rang the bell with the other and I tried and failed to get free of him. After the last flurry, when lots of people bought double rounds, Dad called time with a single ring of the bell. We threw white tea towels over all the pumps and left the bar area so we didn't have to keep saying no.

Our duties finished, my mother drove us down to the Rainbow, a one-storey snooker club on scrubland about a mile out of the village that had a disco every Friday and Saturday night.

'Have fun, be good,' she said as we got out of the car.

We headed to the bar and Matty bought us drinks. He was doing paid work experience at Drax power station with Fairclough Engineering and was flush with cash. He was getting £120 a week, which seemed like riches, and he was also being paid, as I was, for working in our pub. He bought a pint of lager for himself and a red witch – Pernod, cider and blackcurrant – for me. We were legally underage, of course, but no one was bothered about that. It was generally accepted in the area that everyone over sixteen would drink in pubs.

I wish I could remember more – who we talked to, whether or not we danced. The music that would have lured me onto the dance floor then would have been the Cure, Soft Cell, the Smiths, the Pogues. If 'Love Cats' or 'Tainted Love' had come on while we were there, I doubt I would have resisted. We might have danced together. Matty standing tall, not moving much, me twirling around him.

We didn't stay together the whole time. We knew everyone – many of them drank in our pub – and we peeled off from each other to talk to various friends before circling back again. I would have been cuddling him because I always was. People often thought we were girlfriend and boyfriend, which amused us both. 'No,' I'd laugh, 'he's my brother.'

At some point one of our customers offered me a lift home. I asked Matty if he wanted to come. He said no.

This is the moment. If I could go back in time and force him to come with me then everything would be different. Of course I know that's impossible. I just wish I could tell her, the girl with the henna-red hair in charity-shop clothes, to write down everything that happened. *Write it down*, I'd say. *You won't want to – you'll think every detail will be burnt onto your brain forever. You don't know this, but you'll forget.* You'll forget what you talked about, who you chatted to, whether you danced. For some years you'll remember what Matty said as he turned down the lift, you'll be able to see his lopsided grin, the last time you saw his handsome face animated like that, but then you'll forget. You won't be able to see him. You won't be able to remember him. You'll start to doubt that you did go and offer him a lift. You'll start to worry that his response was so perfectly ironic that you made it up, that you dreamt it afterwards, that you never bothered to find him to offer him the lift, or that you looked for him but didn't try very hard. So maybe it was all your fault, and even though you won't really think this could be true, it will worry you down the years that you can't remember it, or rather that you have overremembered it, overplayed it to the point where it has jumped out of reality and become a fiction.

When Matty and I were little we had a Christmas record

we danced around to on which most of the songs had lyrics but 'Frosty the Snowman' was instrumental.

'Why doesn't Frosty have any words?' we had asked our father, who, never one to resist a tease, told us that it was because we had played it so much that we had rubbed the words off. For years we thought this was true and feared that the words in the other songs we liked would disappear with overuse. We kept a strict ear out to detect if they were getting fainter.

Now I know that words don't rub off songs through overuse, but I also know that memory *is* altered to the point of destruction by overplaying.

We were at the Rainbow. I was offered a lift. I went to find Matty and asked him if he wanted to come with us. He was leaning against the pool table, his long fingers wrapped around a pint glass. He was wearing jeans, a brown leather jacket and his favourite T-shirt of the moment, white with *The The* in big red letters.

'No,' he said, grinning, 'I'll hang around here. I might get lucky.'

And I threw him a half-smile, an eyebrow raise, a 'what an arrogant fucker you are' head-tilt, and I walked out of the Rainbow and into the car.

The next time I saw Matty he was lying in the road. And he never, in any sense of the expression, got lucky again.

IN TROUBLE

It was about one in the morning when I got home from the Rainbow. The pub was dark and my parents were in bed. I climbed the back stairs, walked past Matty's room and on to my own. I undressed, pulling the ribbons from my hair, looking around at the sage and lilac walls. I got into bed. What did I do? What did I think about before the events of that night shunted everything else out of the way? Maybe I listened to a mix tape or played a record on my record player, which was black with green and purple buttons. Matty had the same one, presents from our parents the previous Christmas. Did I read? It seems likely. I read everything from Jane Austen to Jilly Cooper. I had recently discovered Julian Barnes at college and wanted to study French so that I could live in an attic in Paris and read Flaubert in his own language. I loved the thought of myself as someone who read novels in French.

Of course, back then reading was still a pleasure and not a defence. This was the last night I wouldn't fear closing my eyes for what I might see. The last night I wasn't in terror of what might happen by the time I woke up.

I was drifting off to sleep when I heard someone shouting outside in the car park. Nothing unusual about that.

Customers often pitched up in the middle of the night looking for their wallets or keys or wives. I opened my window
to see what was going on. The man below didn't look mad
or drunk. He was standing next to his car. The headlights
were on and I could see a woman in the passenger seat.

'Is this where Matthew Mintern lives?'

'Yes. I'm his sister.'

'You'd better come then, he's in trouble.'

Trouble. It was a worrying word, but a small one. I pulled
on all the clothes I'd just taken off and felt a rush of adrenaline that was not unpleasant. No need to wake my parents.
I could sort out whatever it was. Some prank. Some schoolboy silliness. Nothing that couldn't be smoothed over by
a sympathetic older sister. Matty would be grateful. I'd be a
little bit cross with him but then we'd have a laugh about it.
Maybe tell the parents, maybe not.

I picked up my keys, grabbed my handbag and flew down
the back stairs and out into the car park. The man started
driving as soon as I climbed into the back seat. He told me
that Matty had been knocked over by a driver who did not
stop. The man and his girlfriend had been in the car behind.
They'd stopped, found out Matty's name from the girls he
was walking with, called an ambulance from the phone box
at the edge of the village and then headed on to the pub.

I knew immediately that this was bigger than anything I
could have imagined. I wished I'd woken my parents, but it
was too late to change that now.

When we pulled up in the road, I saw crowds of people
in the headlights, all the same people who had been at the

Rainbow and were walking home along the same road. They parted and I floated through them. I heard people say, 'That's his sister.'

Matty was lying in the road. He looked so long; his body was covered with coats. A girl we knew called Vicky told me he was unconscious, that she had put him in the recovery position. I knelt next to him, touched his forehead, stroked his cheek with the back of my fingers. His eyes were closed. There was no damage to his face. I couldn't see any blood. I felt for a pulse. Found it. Kept my fingers wrapped around his wrist so I could feel the evidence of his life.

One of the girls he had been with told me that a car had come out of nowhere. They'd been walking along, the three of them, Matty on the outside, and suddenly he wasn't there any more. Then his body had crashed back onto the road in front of them and the car had sped off into the distance.

'He gave me his jacket to wear,' she said, through tears. 'He gave it to me because I was cold.'

Lots of girls were crying. There was a whiff of drunken hysteria in the air and I knew I must stay calm and not submit to it. Vicky and I made people stand back, so they were not crowding in on Matty. Some of the men had formed a circle facing the other way, ready to warn oncoming traffic.

Sirens, flashing lights. When the ambulance arrived I could tell from the demeanour of the men how serious it was. They scooped Matty onto a stretcher and in through the back doors.

'You're his sister? Hop in, lass.'

They were so quick, so deft. One of them sliced through Matty's T-shirt with what looked like a set of shears. The red letters of *The The* could no longer be made out as the whole T-shirt was soaked with blood.

'But I can't see any cuts,' I said. 'Why is there so much blood?'

'It's coming from the back of his head, lass,' said the ambulance man. I felt like I'd been punched in the stomach. The man gave me little jobs to do, showed me how to stick the pads onto Matty's chest, how to clip on the wires.

The driver was on the radio. 'We've got a bad one, here,' he said. 'I think we're talking Pinderfield's.'

I knew Pinderfield's was a big hospital near Wakefield.

The other man explained that we'd go straight to Ponte-fract Hospital so Matty could be stabilized and assesssed before being transferred somewhere bigger.

'Keep talking to him, love,' he said. 'Keep him with us.'

I talked and talked and talked. I told Matty everything would be OK. I told him about the man coming round to the car park at the back of the pub.

'If he'd gone to the front door, he'd have got Mum and Dad. I should have woken them up. I'll phone them from the hospital.'

I had a feeling that Matty had taken a bit of a shine to Vicky and I babbled at him about this being an extreme way to get her attention.

I was still talking when we arrived at Pontefract and he was wheeled away from me. I wanted to go with him but they wouldn't let me.

'I need you to help me fill in some forms, love,' said a nurse, putting an arm round me.

'Good luck, lass,' said the ambulance man.

I sat in an office. I told the nurse that Matthew Peter Mintern was sixteen and lived at the Bell and Crown in Snaith. I gave her the names of my parents as his next of kin.

'I have to tell them,' I said.

The nurse let me use their office phone. I picked up the chunky receiver and dialled the number, stopping when there was still one digit to go. I thought how my parents would be surprised to hear me on the phone when they assumed I was in my bedroom across the corridor, that they only had a few seconds left of sleeping in happy ignorance of what had happened to Matty. I couldn't leave it any longer. We both needed them. I dialled the last number, a '9', and imagined the shattering of the silence in their bedroom.

'I'm at Pontefract Hospital with Matty. He was knocked over. They say it's very serious.'

My lip wobbled a bit on 'serious', but it was a calm and efficient conversation.

I went to the entrance of A&E to wait for them to arrive. A group of men who had been in a fight were kicking off because they'd been hanging around for a long time, and a nurse told them off. 'This young lass's brother has been knocked down and that's why we don't have any time for you,' she said. They were instantly well behaved. One of them bought me a cup of tea from the machine, and they gathered around me, their big, bloody faces full of kindness and concern.

My composure vanished the moment my parents appeared. We sat on the bolted-down plastic seats, and I sobbed into my mother's shoulder while my father wrapped his arms around her. After a few minutes we were taken to see Matty. He was lying on a bed with his eyes closed, a collar around his neck and an oxygen mask over his face. There were smears of dried blood on his upper chest and face but he looked reassuringly normal.

'He's a big lad,' said Dad. 'He'll get over a knock like this.'

The doctor told us Matty had a serious head injury and was being transferred to Leeds General Infirmary. That a surgeon was waiting for him there. We followed the ambulance in the car, and I lay down on the back seat, stared at the motorway lights through my tears, and thought of all the times we had driven from Yorkshire to Cornwall at night to see my grandparents. Matty and I would share the back seat together top to toe. One of my earliest memories is how we used to bend our knees and put the soles of our feet together, pretending to be riding a bike against each other.

Matty was whisked away as soon as we got to Leeds so we didn't see him. I was distraught, but Mum told me that we didn't want to be getting in the way, that any time we spent with him would delay surgery, would delay fixing him. This calmed me down a bit. We were shown to a little room with a table and chairs, a kettle and an ashtray, and drank tea for what felt like hours and hours. I noticed a Guinness stain on the bottom edge of my cream shirt, knew that it would have happened as I'd leaned over the pump at work earlier, and thought how much the world had changed in the lifetime of that little stain. I smoked. I had never smoked in front of my parents before, but now that little deceit belonged to another universe. There was a smear of blood on my handbag. It was a big brown patent-leather old lady bag that I'd found in a charity shop. I called it Gladys. How stupid, I thought, to give a handbag a name, how childish – I'll never call it Gladys again; and then looked down to see the bloodstains on my hands. I didn't want to wash them. I had been Lady Macbeth in our school play and had used her monologues for my GCSE drama exam. I thought of her, unable to wash the phantom blood from her hands.

'If Matty dies,' I thought, 'I'll never wash my hands again.'

We were taken to another room, the family room in the intensive care unit, and the surgeon told us that he had removed a clot from Matty's brain and a piece of his skull to allow for swelling. It was too early to say if the operation had been successful or what the future might hold for Matty.

'I've saved your son's life, Mr Mintern,' the surgeon said. 'We don't know yet whether that was the right thing to do.'

'Will he be able to walk?' I asked.

He looked at me with weary eyes. 'We don't know anything at this point.'

He told us that Matty would be purposely sedated for at least forty-eight hours. He needed to rest – they didn't want him waking up yet. We could see him shortly.

We carried on waiting in the little room, and I curled up into a ball on the sofa and cried. I still couldn't believe what had happened. Another family arrived – the parents and girlfriend of a man in his mid-twenties called Alex. Alex's girlfriend had come home from her nightshift as a nurse to find him collapsed by their bed.

'I thought he was drunk,' said the girlfriend. Her face was blotched and swollen with tears. I realized I must look like her, must be wearing the same stunned expression.

'I can't believe I thought he was drunk. "Get up," I said, and I was shaking him. And then I realized.'

Finally a nurse took us down to Matty's bed at the bottom end of the intensive care unit. His head and arms were swathed in white bandages, his chest was bare and there were orange stains on his skin, which the nurse told us was iodine from the operation.

I watched his chest rise and fall. I watched the monitor showing the beat of his heart. Forty-eight hours, I thought. A full two days to endure this uncertainty of whether he will live or die.

My only fear at this point was that he would die. I'd been terrified of that since getting in the car with the man outside the pub. Would he die before I got to him, would he die in the ambulance, would he die at Pontefract, would he die in the second ambulance, would he die in surgery? I knew other boys, other young men who had died. There was William, a boy I was at school with who had come off his motorbike, and sweet, gentle Garry, one of our customers, who had been kicked to death by a gang in sleepy Rawcliffe in what had turned out to be a case of mistaken identity.

And Rory, another customer and family friend, whose car had come off the road not far from the scene of Matty's accident. I was used to the notion that young men die tragically and suddenly. I'd even had a dream the week before that Matty died in a motorbike accident. I had never heard the expression 'head injury', I had no concept of brain damage, except that sometimes babies are born that way. I saw things only in binary terms. Dead or alive. All I cared about was that Matty lived.

At 10 a.m. we decided to go home. The pub needed to be opened at 12. As Dad drove and Mum rested her hand on his knee, they made a plan. Dad's priority would be the pub, because more than ever now we would need the money and couldn't afford to let the pub slide. Mum's priority would be Matty. I said I would help with both.

When we got back, Dad did the cellar work, and Mum cashed up and emptied the slot machines; the usual Sunday morning jobs. I had a bath. Polly sat on the bathroom floor and watched me with her big, brown, sad eyes.

'It'll be all right,' I told her. 'He'll be all right.'

I washed Matty's blood from my hands. He was not dead, he had not died in surgery, he would not die. I was already a bit ashamed of my earlier drama-queenery. I couldn't have blood on my hands – I had to work the bar with my dad, as I did every Sunday lunchtime. I didn't wash the blood off Gladys, though, and my orange trousers would always bear bloodstains on the knees from where I'd knelt on the road. I would never mention this to anyone, but would find a macabre enjoyment in the secret tribute every time I wore them.

Mum went back to the hospital, Dad and I opened the pub. We cried all the way through the lunchtime service, and so did many of our customers. The news was flying around the village and people were coming in in streams to ask questions about Matty.

I stood washing glasses. There was a technique to it: you took the circular tray of clean glasses out of the dishwasher, put it on the side and put the next tray of dirty glasses in. Pint pots went straight onto the shelves, half pints on top of the dishwasher, and the rim of each one needed to be wiped with a tea towel in case of lipstick before being put back. I picked the half pints up by their bottoms, four in each hand. As I put them on the other side of the bar by the till, I rested my hand on the warmth of the upturned glass and felt a bolt in my tummy that almost knocked the breath out of me. *Everything is different now*, I thought. Don't forget, don't be lulled by this satisfying, familiar task. Everything is different now.

All the customers wanted to buy us drinks.

'Have one for yourself,' they said, thrusting notes at us.

'I won't, thanks,' said my dad. 'We'll be heading back to the hospital after last orders. I'll take a drink off you when our boy is better.'

The hours inched on. We sat and watched Matty breathing. The other young man, Alex, died. He'd had a massive brain haemorrhage, it turned out, and there was nothing the doctors could do. He was pronounced brain dead and the ventilator was switched off. I could hardly look at his girl-friend as they said goodbye to us and wished us luck. I couldn't bear for her to see my relief that it was her boy-friend who had died and not my brother.

The nurses told us to talk to Matty; they said he must have been physically very fit to have survived. He was, we said. We told them about his sporting prowess, all those trophies for running and football. About the way he could lift himself onto the roof terrace at the back of the pub just by pulling himself up with his hands. How he would then walk across the roof and through the patio door of our upstairs kitchen, giving anyone who was in there a fright. Surely someone this fit and strong couldn't die? Surely some-one who was loved this much couldn't die?

Two policemen called round to the pub on Sunday evening to tell us that the driver had come forward, and one came back later to take a witness statement from me. I told them about being at the Rainbow. I could hardly choke out the words when I described how Matty had turned down the chance of a lift and decided to stay behind without me.

I slept at the hospital on the Monday night. I sat beside Matty until tiredness overwhelmed me and then, on the way to the room I had been assigned, I found the chapel. I knelt and put my hands together. I was an unbaptized atheist, but I had been to the Catholic school in our village, where I had read at Mass and won the school RE prize. I knew all the prayers, and that the God I didn't believe in was kind.

I said the Our Father, a Hail Mary. I asked for my sins to be forgiven. I asked that Mary, mother of God, prayed for us now and at the hour of our death. I said the Hail Mary again in French. I had learned it on an exchange trip with school and thought it sounded very beautiful.

Je vous salue, Marie, pleine de grâce.

I tried to make up my own prayers.

'If you are there, if you exist, if someone can listen to me . . .'

I did my best, then went off to find the tiny white room and fell asleep on the narrow cot-like bed.

In the morning, I woke up thinking it had all been a dream. I stretched and smiled and gloried in the safe warmth. *It was a dream*, I thought, *just a dream*. And then I sensed something unfamiliar about my surroundings, scratchiness against my chin from a woollen blanket, not my own soft duvet. I opened my eyes. These were not my walls. No sage and lilac, only the unbroken white of the relatives' overnight room. No dream, no respite.

I got dressed and hurried back to intensive care. *Today might be the day*, I thought, *if the scan shows the doctors what they want to see, that they stop sedating Matty. Today might be the day that he wakes up.*

I had not yet learned to be thankful for the absence of nightmares.

YOUTH CRITICAL AFTER COLLISION

A Snaith teenager remains in a critical condition following a horrifying road accident in the early hours of Sunday.

Matthew Mintern (16), whose parents run the Bell and Crown public house in Snaith, was believed to have been walking home along the A654 road when he was in a collision with a car.

Goole police said Matthew was making his way home from the Rainbow Snooker Club in Pontefract Road just before 2am when he was struck from behind by a car and carried some twenty metres along the road before being thrown onto the road surface. He sustained serious head injuries.

Immediately following the collision, police appealed for information and yesterday a driver was interviewed. Police inquiries are continuing.

Matthew has lived in Snaith since last October when his parents, Kevin and Margaret Mintern, took over the Bell and Crown. Previously the family lived in Carlton.

Another motorist who passed the scene called at the public house and told them about the collision.

Following the accident, Matthew was rushed to Pontefract Infirmary and then transferred to the intensive care unit at Leeds Infirmary.

His parents maintained a vigil at his bedside, where his mother was as we went to press. A hospital spokesman said Matthew's condition was critical.

Times & Chronicle, Goole, 16 August 1990

THE FIRST TEN DAYS

We spent the next few days driving between the hospital and the pub. I could hardly sleep at night, but I always dozed off on the journey there and back. Once my parents decided to let me sleep on and left me in the back of the car a couple of streets away from the hospital. When I woke, hot and groggy from the sun streaming in through the windows, I felt the usual relief that the whole thing had been a nightmare, then faced all over again the terrible realization that no, it was all true. I thought of the range of things that might have happened as I slept. I might have missed him dying. I might have missed him waking up. I hurried onto the ward, but nothing had happened, nothing had changed.

As the drugs that had been paralysing Matty left his body, there were some initial reactions. His hands clenched, his mouth moved. We got very excited, but were told they were just spasms. He was given a tracheotomy; a hole cut into the base of his throat so that the tubes no longer needed to be put down through his mouth. He looked more comfortable, but we realized it meant the doctors were expecting him to need it for some time. I asked a nurse about it and she told me that the tubes down the throat served their purpose in an emergency, but the friction in the airways would mean sores if they were left in for much longer. I was overwhelmed with all the new things I was learning, and why.

The day after the tracheotomy, Matty left intensive care and was moved onto Ward 26. At least we're leaving intensive care, we said to each other. That must be a good thing.

On Saturday, a week after the accident, I woke up at the hospital hoping, as I had hoped every morning, that today would be the day that Matty woke up. Instead, when I got to the ward, his forehead and the top of his head had swollen and were bulging out over his face. I tried to keep calm but kept thinking about what that customer had said about fifty-bob cabbages and crying. The doctors came and took him for a scan. 'If it's fluid,' they said, 'we'll put in a drain.'

It wasn't fluid. It was the brain tissue swelling up, so another set of drugs went up on the pole to drip into him. This was our worst day yet.

My mother and I sat and looked at Matty as we waited for the drugs to start working.

'How would you even describe it?' I said. I was thinking of our customers, trying to work out what to tell them when they asked for news. 'I've never seen anything like this.'

'It looks like something off a Tom and Jerry cartoon,' she said. 'Unreal.'

'Or the Elephant Man,' I said. 'He looks a bit like that, but worse.'

We knew we were failing to find the words.

'Maybe we should take some photos,' said Mum. 'He'll be interested when he gets better, and you're right, we'll never be able to fully explain to him what he looked like.'

'That's a good idea. We could get a disposable camera and save it for him.'

I thought, but didn't say, that if he died we could throw the camera away. If he died we would never want to be reminded of that moment.

I walked into the city centre and bought one from Boots, and we snapped away as the drugs made no difference and his temperature continued to rise. We had to believe that in the future we'd be showing him these photos. We had to have something good to think about as it looked like his brain might burst out of his head.

'Look,' Mum said, pointing to the temperature chart after the nurse had filled it in. We collapsed into hysterical laughter. There was hardly any chart left for his temperature to rise into. Matty was one single tiny square away from being hotter than anyone had ever envisaged that a human being could be.

It took four days for Matty's head to return to anything like its normal shape. As each day passed, he was in less imminent danger of death, yet still did not wake up. We'd seen plenty of films and read plenty of books – we knew it was our job to gaze at Matty's beautiful face until the moment he either died or sat bolt upright in bed and asked what had happened to him. But this wasn't *Sleeping Beauty*. Pretty soon, his tongue was covered in thick yellow fur and there was a stale, sweaty smell hanging around him. The emphasis switched from praying for him not to die, to learning how to look after a body that didn't move in any intentional way.

'Now, Matty,' said a brisk, kind nurse, 'we're going to give you a bath today. Your mum's going to help, and she's going to wash bits of you she hasn't seen since you were a baby.'

I didn't think, given the extreme circumstances, that Matty would mind Mum washing him until he got better, but I knew that if he could speak he'd express a strong aversion to me getting involved. I could imagine the eyebrow-raise and the hard stare, could hear him say, 'You can fuck right off with the cock washing, sis.'

I learned smaller tasks. I helped change his position every two hours so that he didn't get bedsores. I wiped his face, swabbed his mouth, cleaned his tongue and brushed his teeth using special sticks with pink foam heads. Mum told me that when Matty was born, I'd come to visit at the hospital clutching my brand new toothbrush and tried to poke it into his mouth to clean his non-existent teeth.

'That's lovely,' said a nurse who overheard. 'It's a really good idea to tell him lots of stories that he's in or about people he knows.'

'Tell us how you and Dad met,' I said to Mum. 'Tell us how we came to exist.'

Matty and I had always loved this story. We were fascinated that our father was an orphan and his family had been very poor. That the Christmas after his mother died, when he was eight, he'd hung up a stocking but got nothing in it. We liked his tales of truanting. He'd stopped going to school because he was teased for being dirty, and when he was fifteen he'd run away from his aunt's house and joined the merchant navy. Three years later, covered in tattoos, he'd sailed into Falmouth and met our mother on Custom House Quay.

It had been a local scandal. This scarcely literate Irish sailor knocking up the head girl of the grammar school. Our granny wanted Mum to get an abortion, but she wouldn't do it. Mum told us how she'd loved Dad because he was so different. She was in thrall to his lilting voice. When they'd walked up Spernen Wyn together, she couldn't take her eyes off him and had walked smack bang into a lamp post.

Do you remember, Matty, that night out with the parents and Mum's friend from school, Viv, in the Bon Ton Roulet in Falmouth when you were still hungry and had another corn on the cob instead of a pudding, and Viv kept saying I was a love child, a child of love, and we both made sick noises?

We told him stories from the pub, reminding him that he'd found out it was for sale and said 'Why don't we buy it, Dad?' as we were all in the Chinese takeaway next door waiting for our dinner 'B' for four to be ready. We talked about how Dad had recently had another narrow escape at work at Maltby pit – in his time he'd fallen between two ships in Rotterdam, and had been crushed between the underground wagons at Mount Wellington mine in Cornwall – and thought he'd used up his nine lives and how it was time for a different sort of job. We talked about how exciting it had been to move into the pub and get to know all the customers and their funny ways and stories. We told him that Dick was in trouble after being caught sneaking a look at the *Racing Post* when he was at a wedding with his girlfriend, about Stuart's wife hitting him over the head with an ashtray when he'd come home late and drunk, and about how Gilly had put his false teeth into someone's pint pot when they went to the loo.

Mum read the paper to him, and when I was alone with him I'd remind him of secrets and naughtiness.

Do you remember that time we were hanging around at the train station and you were trying to roll a joint as I sheltered you from the wind, but a sudden gust blew it all away and we walked home without getting stoned? . . . Do you remember the time I was caught smoking in the boys' toilets at school and the teacher said that for an intelligent girl I did some stupid things? . . . Do you remember when I drank all that vodka on the French exchange trip and passed out? The last thing I remember is your face. You were crying. You hardly ever cry but you cried then . . . Do you remember when you and your mates drank all that Blue Label Vodka upstairs and you were OK but Justin was sick in the bath and Lee had to go to hospital? . . . Do you remember that night when we were both working behind the bar and you told Terry off when he said I had a big mouth? I was amazed at you. He's so much older, dominant, the sort of man who likes to boss people around. He got right up close to you, and said, 'Don't think you can treat me like a cunt and get away with it.'

And you said, 'Watch yourself with my sister and you won't have a problem with me.'

I asked you about it later. I said, 'I can't believe you were so cool with Terry.'

You laughed and said, 'I was fucking shitting myself, but you can't let people like that see that you're scared of them.'

I looked down at him, not in any position now to look after himself, let alone me. I squeezed his hand. *Thank you for that. I'll look after you now for a little while.*

I reminded him how we used to fight. *Do you remember our last ever physical fight, which was also the first one you ever won? It was in the kitchen at Almond Tree Avenue. We were twelve and thirteen, maybe, and we were arguing about the washing-up. I threw a milk jug at your head, and even though I missed, you pushed me onto the floor and kicked my head into the corner of the kitchen cabinets until it really hurt, and we never fought again . . . Do you remember that time you were pissed off with me for being noisy and boisterous at your school fete? You said my bright mustard tights and denim shorts looked ridiculous and said you wished I'd fuck off and stop being so annoying.*

I talked to him about times he'd made me cross, usually when he'd left chores undone because he knew I'd do them rather than annoy our parents, and I told him he was forgiven. *But don't think you can do it again when you're better.*

One day I took in *Rats,* the James Herbert novel that Matty had been reading before the accident. I was reading out a scary section and enjoying putting lots of oomph into doing the voices – a couple were going into the woods for sex but it was clear something bad was about to happen – when a nurse stopped me.

'I wouldn't read him anything frightening. It might get into his dreams.'

She told me about a man who'd read a book about snakes

to his wife when she was unconscious, and when she was better she told them that she'd kept hallucinating snakes.

After that, I didn't want to say anything sad, scary or difficult to Matty, though I was fascinated and hopeful that surely this must mean there was something swirling around inside his head. I brought in the complete scripts of *Fawlty Towers*, which I'd given him for Christmas. We used to enact it together. He'd be Basil and I'd be Sybil, though he also liked to make me be Manuel.

Remember how you made me be Manuel, Matty? Not just doing the play, either – you'd sneak up on me anywhere and try to whack me on the forehead with a spoon . . . Remember that thing we used to do that we got off a Jasper Carrott routine? It was a way of letting each other know that we thought the person we were talking to was a dickhead. We just had to very lightly touch the centre of our foreheads with our finger and then catch the other's eye.

Ten days had passed since the accident. Ten days of sitting by Matty in hospital wondering if we were imagining a tiny bit of movement behind his left eyelid. He had loads of visitors. All his friends and lots of our customers would come and tell him stories. His friend Justin had organized a 'Get Well Soon' card from Manchester United football club. We pinned it up on the wall above him along with all the others, and tied 'Get Well' helium balloons to the frame of his bed. Then we went home to serve behind the bar and try to find the words to answer our customers' questions.

The fireplace in the pub was full of flowers for Matty. Upstairs had become a barren place. We hardly lived there any more, only passing through to eat, wash and sleep. The fridge was full of food people had brought for us. The landlady of the Downe Arms, the pub across the road, came over with a casserole every day. People were taking turns taking Polly out for walks. She looked sad all the time.

One day at home I was walking past Matty's bedroom door when I realized I'd started to miss him. I didn't miss him for the very first few days while I was terrified he might die, and after that I didn't think to miss him, the way I hadn't missed him the year before when we went on separate holidays for a week. But now, standing by his bedroom door in our empty home, I was full of longing for him. I missed him appearing over the roof to startle me at the kitchen door. I missed the way he sat by the toaster eating a whole loaf of toast and peanut butter as we chatted. I felt weak and sad. I sat on his bed, looked at the POLICE, SLOW sign that he'd pinched from the roadworks around the corner, looked at the traffic cone he'd drawn a face on with black marker pen. I thought of the way he used to put the cone on his head and dance around. It used to make me laugh so much and now I was crying hard at the thought of it. I looked at his records and put on 'Wish You Were Here' by Pink Floyd. I remembered us sitting in this room listening to that song and imagining ourselves as lost souls in a fish bowl. I'd drawn a pair of intertwined goldfish on his jeans. It could only have been a few weeks ago, but it felt like years.

The brown bag with his clothes in that the police had brought back to us was on the bed. It looked like a potato sack and had a reference number written on it in black marker pen. I wondered if Matty was wearing the goldfish jeans on the night of the accident and had a look, but of course we'd never got his jeans or his T-shirt back because they were cut from him. I sat and held his leather jacket, his brogues, his wallet and the silly sovereign ring that I'd thought was ridiculous but he'd liked wearing. There was blood on the jacket from where the girl he'd lent it to had put it over him as he lay in the road. I looked in his wardrobe to see if I could find the jeans with the goldfish drawing on, but I couldn't. He must have been wearing them. I thought of the intertwined goldfish, separated, sliced through as his jeans were cut.

I wish you were here, I thought. I'm a lost soul without you. I thought of him lying in hospital, starting to heal so that he would wake up and come back to us. I wish you were here, I thought. You will be, you will be.

That day, Matty's eyes started to open at the rate of a couple of millimetres a day. It was a start.

STAR PUPIL BATTLES FOR LIFE
AFTER HIT-AND-RUN

A teenager with a brilliant academic career ahead of him is fighting for his life in a Leeds hospital. Matthew Mintern, 16, was the victim of a hit-and-run driver at Snaith as he walked home from a disco last weekend. The driver of the car has since been traced and questioned by the police about the incident. Matthew's family are keeping a constant vigil at the bedside of the boy who has everything to live for. The bright teenager suffered severe head injuries in the accident which has shocked his school pals and the villagers in the close-knit community of Snaith. And his father, Kevin, landlord of the Bell and Crown pub in the Market Place, spoke of the brave fight being put up by his son who was a star pupil at his local high school. 'This accident has turned our lives upside down. But he is a powerful, strong-willed lad who is very physically fit. If anyone can pull through all this he can.' Matthew remains in a critical condition in Leeds Infirmary but is now breathing off the ventilator. He has started to move his eyes and his limbs.

Yorkshire Evening Post, 16 August 1990

'COMA BOY'

Two and a half weeks after the accident, Matty got the best GCSE results in his school. BBC Look North came to the hospital and interviewed Mum. She told them that Matty's eyes were starting to open, and then the story was picked up by the newspapers. Lots of them referred to him as 'coma boy' and some of them reported that on being told his results by my mother, Matty opened his eyes and smiled at her. This wasn't true. His eyes had started to partly open, but there was no response that indicated any awareness of his grades.

People were turning up at the pub full of joy, ready to congratulate us, and we had to tell them that no, the newspapers were wrong. There had been no miracle. But it was early days and we were still all convinced that we would get one. Despite the misunderstanding, it felt good to have lots of people talking about Matty and hoping for his recovery.

We took the exam results, the concrete, impartial evidence of how bright Matty was, as a point in his favour. How could the God that none of us believed in want to let this talented young life go to waste? We looked at those A grades, at all the interest in them, and were reassured that Matty would survive because he deserved to.

'He's a big lad. He'll get over a knock like this,' Dad had said on the night of the accident. My dad, veteran of close shaves, no stranger to hard physical knocks. He'd been in and out of danger all his life, so of course he didn't believe that his son could be so easily snuffed out.

'It can't be right,' said our head barmaid Carol, shaking her head. 'It can't be right that a lad like that won't get better.'

The story was reported in the Irish papers, too, so all my dad's family were ringing up and pledging their prayers. There was another flurry of flowers, and cards would arrive in the post to let us know that Mass had been said on Matty's behalf. We were all quite moved by this.

'We'll take anything, at this point,' Dad said, his atheism temporarily on hold.

I found it comforting to think that across the Irish Sea people were talking about Matty and caring about what happened to him.

We made a collage of the news stories and pinned it up above Matty's bed at the hospital so that everyone could see what he was like and how much was at stake. We wanted the nurses and physios to know that his headmaster thought he was an Oxbridge certainty; the nurses seemed a little less keen on treating people who were there through their own fault or stupidity. There was a young man who'd been injured when he fell through the roof trying to break into his old school, and the nurses were brusquely disapproving of him. We didn't want that for Matty.

One evening, Matty's friend Didge came to visit while we

were having some tea in the canteen. Matty and I had been friends with Didge since we'd moved to Yorkshire and he was always sleeping over at our house and coming on holiday with us. His father was the caretaker at Carlton Towers, the stately home in the village next to Snaith that we'd come to live in before moving to the pub. Didge and Matty had bought an old grey Fiat 500 for £100 and taught themselves to drive it off-road on the Towers' land. I loved going up to the Towers as I was allowed to have a look in the enormous library and at the priest's hole. Lots of the novels I read featured a priest's hole, and it set my imagination alight to see a real one and know that men had hidden in it.

We came back from the canteen to find Didge sitting down at the wrong bed, holding the hand of the wrong brain-damaged patient, telling him stories about the Fiat. We all made a joke of it, but it was an uncomfortable truth that they looked the same, these young men with shaved, bandaged heads lying there not doing anything. If their eyes were open they had no expression, which made it difficult to tell them apart. So we pinned up Matty's school photo, the one all the papers used, the one with his lovely grin. We were intent on demonstrating his personality for him, as he couldn't do it for himself. *Look at that lovely smile*, we thought. *Who wouldn't want to work extra hard for the chance of seeing that lovely smile again?*

A new patient came to the bed opposite. He was a bit older than Matty and his full head of black, curly hair proclaimed he hadn't had brain surgery, but his legs were in plaster and he'd had a tracheotomy. His mum told us he'd been in a motorbike accident and that his lungs were punctured. He lay surrounded by cuddly toys brought for him by his large, noisy family, who came in droves to pet him and wail over him. His eyes were open; he looked sleepy but aware.

'They're treating him like a baby,' whispered Mum. 'We mustn't let that happen to Matty.'

It's impossible to speak with a tracheotomy, but after a few days of watching the boy look increasingly frustrated and bored, my dad said to the boy's mum, 'He looks like he wants to say something. Why don't you get him some paper and a pen?' So they did, and he wrote, 'Bring me some fags and tell my sister to fuck off.'

There was great hilarity and relief at his recovery, but I couldn't help begrudge it just a tiny bit. It didn't seem fair. What had that family done to deserve it? They hadn't been attentive or responsive, they hadn't even noticed he wanted to communicate. Here we were, all reading up on the latest occupational therapy theory, looking for the first little sign that we would see that smile again, and so far Matty hadn't done anything except open his eyes.

We were learning everything we could about Matty's care. Unable to swallow safely, he was fed with a creamy liquid called Ensure that went into his tummy via a nasal gastric tube. One end of the tube hung out of his nostril, secured with micropore tape. Before each feed we needed to check that the other end of the tube was in his stomach and had not got displaced into his airway. We would draw up a small amount of fluid from his stomach with a syringe and test it with litmus paper. Pink for acid meant the tube was in the right place and the Ensure could then be decanted into a bottle and dripped into him. He was very gaunt and was prescribed 3,000 calories a day, given via several feeds. A red medicine called Epilim was added to the mix, making it the colour of strawberry milkshake. This was to mitigate against epilepsy, which was common after a head injury. There was a little switch on the line to control the flow: too fast and he might vomit it back, too slow and we couldn't get enough in. The tube was changed quite regularly, and in time Mum learned how to do that too. She asked a nurse to do it to her, so that she knew how it felt.

'Oh, it's horrible,' she said. 'I just wanted to gag all the time. Poor Matty.'

We realized that as he didn't make any response to the tube going in, he must not be able to feel it. While we were glad he wasn't in pain, it was disappointing to realize how little awareness he had about what went on inside or around him.

Matty had no control over his bladder or bowels. At first he'd been catheterized, but now he had a convene sheath fitted to his penis, which was like a condom with an open end attached to a bag by a tube. The convene was changed daily but would often spring off when he was moved, or had a wee, so we became expert at changing a wet bed and I had to get over my squeamishness at seeing him naked. It wouldn't help Matty, I thought, for me to make a fuss about how horrible and undignified it all was for him. Better to pretend it was normal. We would roll him onto his side, wash him, pull the soiled sheet from under him and fit the clean one, roll him back onto the clean sheet and whip out the dirty one. While he was in bed we kept him without underwear as it was much easier to deal with a wet or soiled bed if we had no pants to get off and on.

Bathing involved getting him into a hoist by using a large sling like a portable hammock. We would get the sling under him in the same way as changing the sheet, and then the loops were fitted to a hoist and he was transported to the bathroom. The hoist was wheeled over the bath and he was lowered in. We bathed him every day.

Physiotherapists came most weekdays to collect Matty and take him to the department. They would start by sitting him on the edge of the treatment table, a physio kneeling behind him with their arms around him. There would be at least two physios and two of us, and together we would heave him up into a standing position. He had no muscle tone at all, so we all had to hold on tight: knees, feet and hips. The physios were always amazed how tall he was. Once, when he had been constipated for a few days, the act of getting him into an upright position activated his bowels and he did an enormous poo. He had floppy boxer shorts on, so Mum just got a yellow bag (yellow bags were for special bins and had to be used for that sort of thing), fished it out of the bottom of his boxer shorts, put it in the bin and carried on with the session.

We worked too with the occupational therapists, and had a 'box of tricks' for working on Matty's senses. There were different fabrics from fur to sandpaper to rub against his skin, little bottles of smells to waft under his nose, safe ways of letting him taste, including a Polo mint on a string and a Fisherman's Friend wrapped in a muslin bag. We wheeled him out onto the corridors to expose him to different sights and sounds, and even into the small hospital garden when the weather was fair. We learned how to feed him small amounts of puréed food, and had a feeding cup to give him little sips of drinks. And all the time we talked to him. We talked and talked.

The boy that Didge had sat next to by mistake began to get better. He was eventually able to sit up in bed and was then transferred to a rehabilitation centre. It was wonderful to see, and we hoped that Matty wouldn't be far behind.

'See you there,' we said to his family as we waved them goodbye.

Mum kept a diary and recorded Matty's progress – first sound, first yawn, even first slight erection. All these were signs of new things happening in his brain. We thought he would like to read the diary when he got better. We made a pact that we would focus on hope.

But the doctors were concerned by Matty's lack of progress and a scan confirmed hydrocephalus, a build-up of fluid on the brain. We could actually feel it because his head was often puffy where the piece of skull had been removed. It was one of the things we noticed and commented on when we arrived each day, whether the area was convex or concave. Concave looked odd – a four-inch crater at the side of his head – but no swelling was a good sign. Convex looked better – he looked more normal – but it was bad news. They operated and inserted a shunt which took the excess fluid from the brain into the abdominal cavity. Another tube, but this one was inside his body and couldn't be seen. The doctors told us that for the rest of Matty's life his head must never be below the level of his stomach, so that nothing from his gut could flow back up to his brain. 'No cartwheeling for you, Matty, when you're better,' I said.

During the same operation they also put back the bone flap, leaving him with a horseshoe-shaped dent where the edges didn't quite fit. Dad said it looked as if a loose tile had been refitted without enough grout.

At home, we would try to explain all the things that we were learning to our customers as we served them drinks.

'Is he still on a life-support machine?' they'd ask.

'No one in a hospital uses the term life-support machine. It's not as simple as that. He breathes by himself, he's no longer on a ventilator, but all his food and liquid has to be pumped into his tummy through a tube in his nose.'

'Is he still in a coma or has he woken up?'

'Well, his eyes can open fully and he has periods of wake and sleep, but you couldn't really say that he's woken up.'

'Can he communicate by blinking?'

'We think so, sometimes. Sometimes we think he'll blink yes or no, but we can't really tell for sure.'

'Does he move?'

'Sort of. But it's all spasms and spasticity. He sort of wrinkles his mouth if he doesn't like something.'

'What does he do all day?'

'He sleeps a lot. Like a really poorly person would. We

talk to him and tell him stories. He has a lot of visitors. He has physio. We've taken in a telly and play him comedy videos. We try to get him to eat and drink tiny bits.'

Misunderstanding abounded. Because we always talked positively and hopefully about Matty, people tended to think he was doing better than he was and were then shocked if they visited him to find that his gaze was either vacant or his eyes locked over to the right, that his skin was deteriorating and that he had spots and blackheads for the first time in his life. When Dad told someone that we'd been walking Matty in physio – a task that involved four people lifting his toneless body to a standing position and gently manipulating him backwards and forwards – the story spread around the village via Chinese whispers until someone came into the pub to say how happy they were that he was walking around on his own and would he be match-fit by the start of the next football season?

September rolled around. I didn't want to go back to my sixth-form college in Scunthorpe. I no longer cared about my academic future and was convinced that Matty would need me for his rehabilitation.

I had always loved school and learning, especially reading. Mum said that when I was a baby I didn't much care for toys but would gum on a cloth A-Z book as though I knew how much books were going to mean to me in the future.

This aptitude for reading could cause trouble. In my first year of school, when we still lived in Cornwall, my teacher, impressed with my ability, sent me in to read to the class above. It was all a bit much: I looked down and watched my wee searching out the cracks between the wooden floorboards. When we moved to Yorkshire a few months later, my new teacher didn't believe that I'd read all the books I said I had and made me start again. In the free choice reading time, when I finished my book and went back for another, she shouted at me: 'You can't possibly have read that. Sit back down and read it properly.'

When I was seven, Dad went to adult literacy classes because he needed to be able to write shift reports. Mum would test us both out of the same big red spelling book every night. I always won and Dad was always proud of me. He talked a lot about the importance of education. He earned a lot of money, but the work was difficult, dirty and dangerous. He'd often tell us that if we worked hard at school, we wouldn't have to work night shifts or spend most of our time in tunnels underground. We weren't convinced by this as his working life seemed very glamorous to us, and we loved it when he came home off nights just as we were waking up and sat, his eyes rimmed with coal dust, telling us tales of what had gone wrong the night before as he ate his breakfast. We adored the men he worked with and it was a massive treat to go over to Selby and see them in the pub. He'd stand us up on a table and we'd sing the Irish songs he'd taught us to great applause.

My favourite place when I was growing up was the library in Snaith. I'd been getting out all the Anne books by L. M. Montgomery, but there was one I hadn't read because they didn't have it. One Sunday evening we were all watching

Mastermind and one of the contestants chose *Anne of Green Gables* and its sequels as her specialist subject. I got all the questions right except the two based on *Anne of Windy Willows*, my missing book. My parents were very pleased, and that Christmas gave me the boxed set so I could own them all myself.

We were teased for having posh voices. Matty developed more of a Yorkshire accent in time, but I never did. This meant later on that I was used whenever anything needed to be said. At the Catholic secondary school we went to in our village, despite our parents being atheists and us being unbaptized, we settled in nicely: the teachers were kind and liked the fact that we were clever. We grew up winning prizes and races. We were captains of sports teams, heads of house, got the lead parts in school plays. We stood up to bullies, looked after the underdogs, had lots of friends, but were also both a tiny bit rebellious. When I got chosen to have lunch with the visiting Tory MP, I wore long red socks, and Matty got into a major row about evolution with an RE teacher who believed in the literal truth of the Bible. We were lucky to be all-rounders – it was a way to survive. On top of that, I started smoking and swearing when I was fourteen as a considered tactic, along with the overuse of eyeliner. I practised the swearing in my bedroom, watching my mouth in the mirror as it formed the bad words. I wanted to be able to carry on being top of the class without committing social suicide. I wanted to be able to go everywhere and do everything. I liked smoking behind the conifers with the bad kids, and I also liked pleasing my teachers. When I left school my RE teacher, a good man, who did not believe in the literal truth of the Bible, sent us all off with a little note. Mine said: 'You have been a continual breath of fresh air in the occasional fish market of school.'

Now all this seemed to have happened in another universe and I couldn't summon any enthusiasm for continuing my education. We were hoping Matty would get better quickly, might only need to have a year or so off, so I wanted to drop out of sixth form now and pick it up again later when he could too. Mum, keen to try to keep things as normal as possible for me, brokered a deal with the college that I'd go back into the lower sixth and repeat the year I'd just done, which meant I could attend as and when I wanted to as long as I did the work, and could therefore spend as much time with Matty as I wanted.

It was weird going back. Scunthorpe wasn't like Snaith, where everyone knew all about Matty. I felt completely separated from my friends and their stories and started to dodge out of conversations because I didn't want to be asked how my summer was.

Everything apart from being with Matty seemed irrelevant. I'd always kept diaries and notebooks, but now I wrote nothing. My words had gone AWOL. I couldn't bear to read the pointless, silly rubbish the old me had written so I tied all my diaries up in two carrier bags and chucked them into the skip at the back of the pub.

Reading was still my friend, though. I read constantly and compulsively, drowning out the sounds of my own thoughts with the noise of other people's stories. I no longer turned out the light before going to sleep – I had to read until the moment my eyes closed. There could be no gap for the demons to jump into.

Mum and Dad wanted me to carry on trying to do normal things as well as visit Matty, so on the first weekend of term I went to a party at a friend's house. There was a girl there who had found a newspaper report about Matty and was showing it to everyone, and she kept asking me questions, all wide-eyed and waving her hands around, clearly enjoying the excitement of it. I felt like an odd kind of celebrity and didn't know what to do with myself or how to be with those people. So I got drunk, and then sat in an armchair in the corner and got really stoned. The walls were tilting, my limbs were heavy . . . In the haze I thought I was Matty. I watched the tears fall onto my shirt, unable to lift a hand to brush them away, and then I was sick all over myself.

After that, I steered away from drugs. Matty and I had always blithely ignored the fact that our parents, permissive in many other ways, hated drugs because who ever does everything their parents want? Now, though, I didn't want to add to their problems. It felt very important that I should be a good daughter. And I didn't want to mess with my own head. I had enough trouble controlling my imagination as it was. I couldn't bear to be brought face to face with my unruly imaginings.

I sat in Matty's bedroom a lot, playing his records and looking out of his window at the beer garden, and one day I noticed that his sovereign ring had been taken out of the brown bag and put on his bedside table with money rolled up in it. I had a closer look. Matty's GCSE results slip was there too, and I realized this was Mum keeping her side of the bargain and rewarding him for his results as she'd always done with both of us. There would be a pre-agreed amount of money for school reports and exams – perhaps £10 per A – and a family trip to the China Palace in Selby to celebrate. I found it unbearably sad, this reminder of how things used to be and how much everything had changed.

I didn't tell Matty about this. There was no room for any complex personal stuff in this new life. He was the prodigy who needed to be saved and I was his devoted sister.

I always talked to Matty as though he understood everything I said, even though there was no evidence to suggest that he did. But how could I tell him how miserable I was without him? How could I complain about anything that was happening to me in the face of the magnitude of what had happened to him? Instead I stayed upbeat and jolly, carried on telling him funny things that happened in the pub, and reached further into our childhood for safe stories:

Do you remember when Granddad used to take us early-morning fishing and we'd creep down the stairs in the dark and toast a piece of bread in the Rayburn before going out into the dark? . . . Do you remember going to see Star Wars *on the big screen in the village hall and you wanting Mum to put my hair in Princess Leia plaits for ever after? . . . Do you remember when we got Polly? Mum came home from work where one of her colleagues had told her of a whole sack of puppies thrown into the river to drown. One of them yapped and yapped and a passer-by jumped in to save them, and only one little one was still alive. A mongrel, obviously, but looking like a black Lab. We begged and begged for her and Mum said we could have her if we looked after her . . . Do you remember when we got the Granada Scorpio and it was the first car in the village to have electric windows and Dad drove it down to the park so all our friends could have a go at pressing the button to put the window up and down? . . . Do you remember playing with your train set? You'd lay the track, make the trains run and do the building, and I'd make up stories about the people who lived in the little houses and the reasons why they travelled . . . Do you remember going swimming on Friday nights in Kellingley? How we could smell the colliery in the air and would always go to the Chinese takeaway on the way home?*

There were moments of light in the darkness. Dad was much better at reading than he used to be, but he still got confused. On the ward, anyone awaiting surgery would have a sign that said 'Nil Orally' put up at the end of the bed. Watching such a sign go up one day, Dad said, 'That Neil O'Reilly moves around a lot, doesn't he?' We had a laugh and it made a good story to take back to the pub.

The pub helped us stay buoyant. We couldn't be miserable because we needed to keep our customers entertained, and after a while I realized that I was better off being downstairs behind the bar pretending to be happy than upstairs alone with my own thoughts.

TUG OF WAR

December. Four months had passed since the accident and there had been no miracle, but by now Matty was showing a tiny level of response: I could get him to move his head round towards me by dancing and singing out of his eyeline. We went to the hospital every day and took in a mirror and a mobile and posters of the periodic table and the solar system to experiment with, holding them up at different distances from him as we didn't know yet whether or not he could see anything with his open eyes.

The feeding was going so well that the nurses had stopped all daytime Ensure feeds, and we were keeping a food chart, although he was still fed Ensure overnight to keep up his calories and hydration. We had even taken him home for the weekend for the first time. The transfer was difficult. We used a small hospital wheelchair and our car – the Granada Scorpio with the electric windows – and neither of them provided adequate support for his toneless body. As we tried to lift him out of the car and into the flimsy wheelchair, we had to put him down and he ended up splayed out in the pub car park like a Saturday-night drunk.

Once we got Matty upstairs and settled, he was responsive. Propped up on the sofa, surrounded by his friends, he was able to move his head to follow voices and movement. So many people called up to see him, and I gave him tiny tastes of lager by dipping my finger into a glass and then patting the drips onto his lips. Polly sat at his feet, tail thumping, not quite able to understand his lack of activity but enjoying the party atmosphere. It was a joyous weekend, and we felt sure he was about to speak to us. The physios commented how much better he was after his visit home, and on Wednesday 5 December they had their best ever session, with Matty raising his head each time the physio asked him to.

Mum was warming up for her darts match the following Wednesday evening when the hospital rang. This had never happened before, and as she went to the phone she was excited, recalling another young man on the ward who, like Matty, had been slow to progress, and who, as his parents were leaving after a visit and were almost out of the door, had said 'Goodnight, Mum.' Could this be the hospital ringing with good news?

It was Rachel, one of our favourite nurses.

'I'm afraid Matthew has had a major epileptic attack. Status epilepticus. We've given him an injection and stabilized him.'

We knew Status epilepticus was life threatening, The doctors had explained it all when they decided to take Matty off his anti-epilepsy drugs in November because they were concerned at his lack of progress and thought that the medication could be sedating him too much. It had seemed worth the risk but now, although they'd saved his life, the fit had reversed the small amount of progress that had been made. No more feeding by mouth, just watered-down Ensure through the tube. No standing at physio, just some-one coming to his bedside and doing some light work to keep his joints and muscles moving. No response, no follow-ing of voices.

The night after was the presentation evening up at Matty's school. He had won the overall Award for Academic Achievement and the English Prize. My parents decided they couldn't face it.

'I'm too tired,' said Mum, 'and Dad is too sad. It will be too much of a reminder of what we've lost.'

'I'll go,' I said. I wanted Matty to have his trophies and I wanted to be able to tell him about them. Mum hugged me and told me how brave I was.

I wore the same green suede jerkin I'd been wearing on the night of the accident and a pair of blue silk flared trousers, and walked up to school with Matty's friend Ian's parents, Mr and Mrs Robinson. They were lovely people and good friends of our family. Mr Rob, as he was known, ran the football team Matty had played in since he was nine. They were called Camblesforth Colts and had become quite good after a few legendary defeats in the early years. I used to go and watch them and tagged along on the trips Mr Rob organized to Hillsborough to see Sheffield Wednesday. Mr Rob wore his distress about Matty very openly, tears brimming in his eyes.

I managed to hold it together as I walked up to the stage to collect Matty's certificates, his trophy and a £10 gift voucher for WHSmith, and shook hands with the headmaster as he said that the whole school was rooting for Matty's recovery. Back in my chair, I remembered all the presentation evenings in the past, all those times we'd both picked up certificates. I'd usually had the lead part in whatever sort of entertainment was being put on for the parents and governors – I'd been Lady Macbeth and Lady Bracknell in the final two years of school – and as I watched the school choir and band, the younger ones nervously playing their recorders, I thought back to the times when I used to get lost playing the recorder and how I'd stop blowing and just move my fingers over the holes, hoping no one would notice. It seemed amazing to me now that I could ever have cared about playing the recorder or learning lines or winning prizes or anything at all.

Awards were given out for attendance, and each child who had not missed a day of school got a certificate. One girl, a friend of Matty's, had not missed a day of school in all five years, so she got a trophy, and then the headmaster presented a bouquet of flowers to her parents, whose two elder children had also been through their entire school careers without missing a single day. I knew this family: they were beautiful, with Irish looks – black hair, pale skin, red lips. I couldn't grasp that they had all not only achieved adulthood but had done so without a single illness. I thought of my parents at home, prevented by everything that had happened from being able to enjoy Matty's achievements, and felt so glad that they hadn't come, to be faced with the contrast between us and the healthiest family in the history of the world.

There was, of course, some drinking afterwards. I went with Ian and the rest of Matty's friends, who treated me with a brotherly respect that moved me, and by the end of the night the other girls and I were crying over how terribly we all felt Matty's absence. He had been massive, in personality as well as size. He had always been central to everything, made everything better and funnier just by being there – there was just an unfillable hole anywhere he used to be. On that, as on many other nights, I cried myself to sleep.

Christmas was coming. Our second Christmas in the pub. The first one had shocked us with the sheer amount of work it brought, but we'd rounded up Matty and all his friends to help with collecting glasses and bottling up.

The hospital agreed that Matty could come home for Christmas. We'd borrowed a bed and a hoist from the hospital. He slept in Mum and Dad's room, and they set an alarm for every two hours to turn him in the night. Each day we would bathe and dress him and move him into the living room so that visitors could call to see him. We'd put him back to bed after last orders.

When carrying him from room to room we used a technique called the Australian lift, where two people make a type of sedan chair by clasping each other's wrists under the patient's bottom. Matty had made some progress again and was back to taking small bits of food, but his main nutrition still came from the Ensure feeds which we would hang from a picture hook above the sofa. There was no shortage of friends and customers willing to sit with him while we worked behind the bar – one chap proudly declared 'he's drunk all that' when the feed had dripped through, as if he was a baby who had finished his bottle.

Following the big fit, Matty was back on epilepsy drugs. They made him very sleepy most of the time, and it was disappointing for his visitors that he was so unresponsive. Everyone secretly hoped that it would be their voice or joke or story that would rouse him back to life.

On Boxing Day there was the annual inter-pub tug of war which attracted crowds of people, and anyone who pulled for the Bell and Crown got a gallon of ale, whether they won or lost. I made up the little brown envelopes, the same ones we used to pay wages, with eight signed raffle tickets, one per pint. Men would be green and shaky afterwards, sometimes throwing up before feeling recovered enough to start cashing in their tickets.

After last orders on Boxing Day night, there was a fight outside and the back windows got smashed. Dad went out and restrained the person responsible, and the next morning the police came round to say that the man wanted Dad prosecuted for assault. The same person made threatening phone calls all through Christmas saying he would burn the pub down with all of us in it, and it felt grossly unfair that we had to cope with this as well as looking after Matty and working so hard, but we didn't really have time to be frightened. We knew that the phone calls would stop when the man lost interest and in the meantime customers were waiting and pints needed to be pulled, so we got some new glass fitted in the broken windows and opened up with smiling faces ready for the next session.

We took Matty back to the hospital on New Year's Eve and then got ready for what was the busiest night of all, but also the last big effort as everything would return to normal the next day. There were crowds of customers, many in fancy dress, and at midnight there was a brief reprieve at the bar when all the customers went out into the street to sing 'Auld Lang Syne' or get off with each other, depending on their age and inclination. I went outside to collect glasses, but first leant against the front wall of the pub smoking a cigarette and watched the drunk, happy, dressed-up people in the street. Lots of people came to hug me, and some of them mentioned Matty. 'Let's hope this will be a better year for you all, lass.'

I finished my fag, picked up the glasses from the street and walked down the alleyway to go in through the back door, passing a gorilla in the beer garden who was relieving himself into a plant pot.

We served up last orders and started on the mammoth task of getting the pub back to rights, which involved mopping up sick in the toilets, unblocking the urinals and sweeping up all the broken glass in the street. As usual, Dad gave himself all the most unpleasant jobs, and when everything was done we sat up with the rest of the staff, giving them drinks to thank them for working so hard. We got drunk really quickly as the adrenaline that had kept us going for the last hectic fortnight flooded out of our bodies, and we talked about New Year's resolutions. All we wanted was for Matty to get better. It had been a fuck of a year.

Dad got super drunk, and Mum helped him up to bed, leaving me to lock up. I let everyone out and lingered a moment in the dark. *1991*, I thought, *what will you bring us?* I climbed the back stairs, too sad to look in on Matty's bedroom, and as I passed the door to my parents' room I saw that Dad was lying on the floor, holding the leg of the empty hospital bed, sobbing. Polly was sitting next to him, her head on one side, looking sad.

I cried and cried myself to sleep, so drunk that I didn't even wake up when I burned my knee on the radiator next to my bed. I still have the scar.

DRIVING WITHOUT
DUE CARE AND ATTENTION

The police prepared a case against the driver who knocked Matty down and on 8 January – my eighteenth birthday – it came to court in Goole and was adjourned.

None of us were in the mood to celebrate my birthday. My parents gave me a card with irises on it and a cheque, but didn't put any words in the card, just a row of kisses. I was glad they hadn't tried to write anything celebratory: the idea that I might have a happy birthday was absurd. One of the ladies in our darts team made me a cake and I got drunk and then sobbed myself to sleep.

Matty's birthday was a month later and we fetched him home for the weekend. Mum and Dad gave him a new cassette player and a clock.

'It should have been a car,' said Mum, 'but there's no point dwelling on what should have been.'

We blew up lots of balloons and all his friends came round. He was responsive, moving his head between his best friend, Ben, on one side and Claire and Sarah on the other and making little moaning noises.

The case came up again on 14 March. The driver was charged with driving without due care and attention and leaving the scene of the accident. He was fined £180.

The magistrate said, 'This was an unfortunate night for both these young men.'

We couldn't get our heads around how he could have said that. My parents were angry and upset, and Mum said, 'We should have wheeled Matty in here. He wouldn't have made that comment if he could see him.'

I just felt sad. I felt sorry for the driver and imagined how I'd feel if I'd done something like that to someone.

The police explained that, unless someone died, the court didn't distinguish between driving into a person and driving into a tree. They also pointed out that we should be grateful that the driver had been insured, because this meant we could get some money from the insurance company for Matty. We could see the logic of this, and we knew we had to follow the process as getting Matty better was going to be a longer and more expensive job than we'd hoped, but we hated even a whisper of the word 'compensation'. The idea that any amount of money could make up for what had happened to Matty was beyond our understanding.

A LONG, TRUE, SAD STORY

We were approaching another summer. Nine months after the accident, Mum and Dad went to a gloomy case conference with the medical staff. Brain scans showed that Matty had had a further bleed and a stroke. There weren't many damaged areas, but those that were, were critical: speech and directed movement. We concentrated on the positive bits. 'Not many damaged areas,' we said. We'd heard that the brain could be taught to forge new pathways. We wanted to keep trying.

The hospital announced that they could not keep Matty any longer as they needed the bed for more hopeful cases, and told us that he wasn't suitable for referral to the specialist rehabilitation unit as he hadn't made enough progress for anyone to build on. It was suggested he be moved to Scunthorpe or Goole hospital, but we made a decision to care for him ourselves at home. At least then we would all be together, and we wouldn't have to worry about what was happening to Matty when we weren't with him.

The hospital supported this decision and fitted a PEG tube directly into Matty's stomach so we no longer had to change it or do the litmus paper test before each feed. Matty looked less medicalized without the tube hanging from his nose, but for us it felt like a backward step. We had hoped he would eventually progress enough to take food and drink through his mouth, but the PEG represented an acceptance of the permanency of his condition. He would have physiotherapy three times a week at Goole hospital, and the head physio at Leeds gave Mum a sealed letter to pass on to the physios there. 'If you open it I don't want you to be upset by the term *vegetative*,' he said. 'It's just a word we use to describe the condition.' Mum didn't open the letter, but it was the first time we had heard that word used about Matty. It was difficult not to be upset by it.

There was much to do to prepare for Matty's homecoming. Not bunting and balloons, but specialist equipment – a ripple mattress that prevented bed sores, a hoist, shower trolley and wheelchair. A district nurse would call, a home help would be there for the morning bath, and a rota of professionals and friends would sit with Matty so that we could carry on working behind the bar.

Once he was home, I spent a lot of time sitting on the sofa with him. I'd put on the comedy videos we used to watch together before the accident. He couldn't be left alone in a seated position in case he coughed and toppled over, so he'd be propped up with a pillow under one of his arms, and I'd cuddle myself around him on the other side, putting my arm across his waist and resting my face against his chest. I'd pull his arm around me and hold onto his long fingers, interlacing them with mine. Sometimes I'd close my eyes and imagine that the accident had never happened. Sometimes

I'd cry, very quietly because I didn't want him to know, and let my tears fall onto his T-shirt.

Only a matter of months ago we'd been sitting on this sofa with one of his friends who'd kept tickling my feet.

'If you're going to try to get off with my sister,' Matty had said, 'don't do it in front of me.'

I'd always felt so proud when he'd referred to me as his sister. I wondered if he still knew that I was, if I existed somewhere in his head.

Once we'd watched a film about the French Resistance and I'd sobbed my way through it while Matty had remained unmoved.

'How could you not cry?' I asked at the end.

'I wouldn't ever cry at something made up.'

'But it was based on a true story.'

'Oh. I might have done, then, if I'd known. It was really sad.'

Now he was stuck in his own long, true, sad story with me there watching it.

In August, a year after the accident, Matty went into a major fit as I sat with him in our usual place on the sofa. It started with a horrible noise like a cross between a shout and a scream, and then his face started twitching and his arms and legs jerked rapidly. His eyes rolled up into his head, leaving only the whites showing, and his lips turned blue. I shouted down to the bar for someone to come up and help me. Mum and Dad had gone to Goole Leisure Centre for a swim and we couldn't get hold of them, but we called the doctor and he called an ambulance.

The ambulance pulled up in front of the pub, sirens wailing and lights flashing, and the men charged up the front stairs, got Matty onto a stretcher and bundled us off to Pontefract Hospital. I was terrified but trying to stay calm – I knew it was possible that Matty could die. There was panic from the medical staff when we got there – I don't think they had seen anything like it before – and they couldn't find a vein to get an intravenous line into his arm to administer the drugs to stop the fit. I kept telling them that they wouldn't, that his veins had hardened, that they needed to try his foot, but they wouldn't listen and kept stabbing at his arms as he flailed around. I couldn't bear to keep watching, so I stood at the window and looked down at the car park through my tears. I was letting Matty down, I knew it – the more upset I got, the less inclined they were to listen to me, but I couldn't control myself. If Mum had been there she would have got the message across. Eventually they gave up on his arms and got a line into his foot, and Matty was stabilized. They discharged him the next day.

Life had changed beyond recognition in the last year, but we felt lucky that he was still there to cuddle and love and hope for. 'At least we've still got our Matty,' said Mum when the little baby of one of our customers died. 'At least we've still got him and can tell him we love him.'

For a while a Catholic priest visited regularly, an old man who struggled with the stairs and always arrived puffed-out and hot. We joked amongst ourselves that we might have to call in another one to administer him the last rites. We hadn't asked for him to call, but as Matty and I had both attended the Catholic school in Carlton before Matty moved to Snaith for his last two years, he probably assumed we were of the faith. We were never quite sure what we were supposed to do – offer him tea, whisky? Cash? Dad was full of bitter memories from his childhood of priests visiting the poorest people and getting money out of them. One day the priest arrived when Mum was trimming Matty's nails. 'If his hair and his nails are growing,' he said, 'there are signs of life.' Another day, arriving particularly out of breath, he asked, 'When did Matthew have his First Communion?' 'He didn't,' Mum said, and we never saw him again.

We also had visits from various lawyers and doctors to assess Matty for the compensation claim and write reports about him. They all diagnosed him as being in a Persistent Vegetative State with no likelihood of recovery, though we didn't believe that and were far from giving up hope. What I found troubling was that the people who came from 'the other side' – the driver's insurance company – were entirely focused on paying out as little as they could, and always behaved as though they wanted to catch us out in some way, though of course there wasn't anything to catch us out on. I couldn't understand why they wouldn't behave honourably and treat us all with a little more respect and compassion. One day, Mum was explaining to a lady sent by the insurance company how her life had changed – that instead of discussing sixth form colleges and university courses with her children, she'd had to give up her career and become an expert in disability equipment.

'Ah well,' said the lady, 'life doesn't always work out how you planned it, does it?'

Eventually the insurance company made an offer. Our solicitor said it was an opening salvo and they were expecting to have to pay much more. My parents had had enough of the whole thing and wanted to settle. Our solicitor told us the insurance company was so surprised by this that they speculated that Matty had died.

'Well,' said Dad, 'at least it's over and we don't have to spend any more time with that shower of shits.'

A more welcome visitor was Mrs Shaw, Matty's form teacher, who had also taught him English. Matty had always been more interested in science, and he'd changed schools because the one we went to in Carlton decided to offer only a general science GCSE rather than physics, chemistry and biology. Once he'd settled in at Snaith, though, and possibly because he was no longer being compared with me, he'd started to love English with Mrs Shaw. 'I could never get cross with him,' she said, smiling through her tears, 'even when he was cheeky. He was so full of charm.'

Not long after Matty came home, Polly died. The joy had gone out of her after Matty's accident, and she pined away. One of our customers took her to the vet for us so she could have a hysterectomy, but she had a heart attack during the operation. When our customer came to tell us about it,

Mum and Dad were out – they had taken Matty to physio – so it was just me. 'I'm so sorry,' she said, crying, 'I know how awful it is to lose a dog – just like losing a child.'

I was worried I might get the giggles. It seemed a ridiculous thing to say, given what had happened to Matty.

At least Polly had had a quick death, I thought. It was the first time I'd allowed myself to consider even for a second that it might have been better if Matty had not lived. I thought about how the old me would have cried buckets for Polly, but that now I had nothing left to give her. All my sadness was for Matty, and I couldn't scare up a tear for his poor dog.

I could feel myself becoming a less pleasant person and was often angry and resentful, though I tried not to show it. I'd stand either behind the bar or out in the pub and fix on a smile as I listened to people who had not had their hearts ripped out by Matty's accident but who somehow felt they had some ownership over it. They'd tell me how dreadful they felt, where they'd been when they heard the news, what their last conversation with him had been about.

'I love that lad like one of my own,' people said. At first I thought that was lovely. He was loved; it was nice that people said it. But I came to hate hearing it. I'd nod and smile, knowing that their own children were safe and that they had no idea what our life had become. 'Really?' I wanted to say. 'Do you think this is your tragedy? Do you think you feel the same way we do? Because if you do, that's insane.'

I hated people who made any sort of reference to God, as though this could possibly be part of some grand design. A religious person said to me, 'This is the sort of thing that tests my faith.' I'm sure it was meant kindly, but I was furious that he had appropriated my brother's pitiful situation to play out his relationship with his God.

There was no pleasing me. I was angry with people who wanted to talk to me about Matty, but also angry when they stopped asking and didn't want to see him. A tragic accident and a coma are exciting, but the prospect of permanent severe brain damage much less so. People didn't want to see him. They had loved him – not quite like one of their own, but they had loved him – and it was distressing for them to see him so transformed. They gradually drifted away.

One morning, I poured a boiling hot kettle over my arm on purpose. I hadn't planned it, but as I stood waiting for the switch to click, I found myself thinking about the idea that physical pain distracts from emotional pain, and just decided to try it.

It was agony. Far worse than I'd thought it would be. My arm was immediately covered in blisters and I could see I'd need to go to hospital, which hadn't really occurred to me. I was wearing the six camel bangles that my dad had brought back from a work trip to Dubai for Mum, and they had heated up and burnt horizontal lines onto my wrist. I phoned a taxi and cried all the way to the hospital because I felt like such an idiot. I didn't dare tell anyone I'd done it on purpose.

The doctor said they might have to cut the bangles off,

and I couldn't bear that my stupidity would lead to the beautiful bangles being ruined so I took a deep breath and pulled them off over the burnt flesh. Then they bandaged me up and I went home. It was a huge inconvenience because I couldn't work my shifts for a few days, and I felt both irresponsible and fraudulent because everyone was so nice to me and I didn't deserve it. Worse, despite the considerable pain in my arm and the shame at having done it, I never felt one iota distracted from the pain in my heart.

I tried, as time ticked on, to learn to live with our new reality. I drank huge amounts, but so did lots of people we knew, and no one really noticed, least of all me. It didn't occur to me that our most regular customers weren't exactly the yardstick for a normal drinking habit.

WAS IT FOR THIS THE CLAY GREW TALL?

The most difficult practical thing for us was getting Matty up and down the stairs, either to go to physio or for fresh air. The back stairs were too narrow, so we had to carry him down the front stairs and out through the pub. On sunny days, we'd take him out into the beer garden and set up him under a sunshade. We left his feet sticking out unprotected once, and his shins got slightly burnt. We rubbed aftersun on, and it reminded me of the time we were on holiday in St Lucia when we were seven and eight and his arms and the very tops of his ears were badly burnt whilst the rest of him that had been underwater in the pool was OK. Matty had been up all night in agony back then. Now he made no reaction.

'You can't carry on like this,' said our customer and friend, Frank. Frank was the first person Dad had met when we'd moved to Yorkshire, and we were very close to him and his wife, Liz. He was a draughtsman. 'Why don't you knock down the garage and build an extension? I'll draw you up some plans.'

Frank said he was worried about both our safety and our backs, not to mention what would happen if some disgruntled customer did come and try to burn the place down, as they always seemed to be threatening to do. He also pointed out that it was bad for trade to be carrying Matty through the pub. We needed our own space and our own garden for him because people didn't want to see him.

This was dreadfully hard to hear, but we knew it was true, and we respected Frank for saying it. I realized that there were two parts to it. If it was an emergency admission, like the epileptic fit, if there was a shrieking ambulance in the street and paramedics running up the stairs to bring Matty through on a stretcher, then that was acceptable and even a bit exciting, a break from routine. But if it was part of the routine, if Matty was being lifted down to be wheeled off for a physio session or out for a walk, if there was no rush and people had the opportunity to see his giant, wrecked body, to look into his vacant eyes, to notice the crater in the side of his head . . . no one in their right mind would want to witness it as they sipped away at their hard-earned pint.

So we decided to knock down the garage where Matty had built his motorbikes, where he and I had discussed the existence of love, and build a special bungalow to house him in its place. But then the local council decided they wanted the land behind the pub for a public car park and put a compulsory purchase order on it. A long battle ensued. Dad rang up BBC Look North, and the same people who'd interviewed Mum about Matty's GCSE results came to film us lifting him down the stairs in a wheelchair. Our customers were fierce on our behalf, organizing a petition and galvanizing support.

Once again Matty was in the papers.

PARENTS' PLEA TO COUNCIL

Battling Snaith parents Kevin and Margaret Mintern presented a 1500-signature petition to Boothferry Council on Monday in a bid to persuade the council to allow them to build special accommodation for their brain-damaged son.

The couple brought to the council offices in Goole their 17-year-old son Matthew, paralysed and brain damaged by an accident. The couple hope the petition will persuade councillors to reverse their decision to purchase compulsorily land at the rear of their public house in order to create a public car park.

Instead the Minterns wish to use a small part of the land, which they own – four parking spaces – to build a single-storey extension where they may care properly for their shattered son.

There was only a receptionist available at the council's offices when the family arrived, accompanied by the friends who had helped to collect the support of more than half of the total population of Snaith and Cowick.

After 10 minutes the mayor's secretary appeared, and was in the process of accepting the petition from a reluctant Mrs Mintern when it was made known that chief executive John Barber was on his way. He was accompanied by the mayor and the borough solicitor when he arrived, and the Minterns were finally able to present their point of view.

This is simply that assertions made on TV and elsewhere that the people of Snaith were adamant in their demand for a car park were unfounded; 1520 of them supported the Minterns' plea for permission to build, on their own land, accommodation for their son.

The last word belonged to Kevin Mintern. He and his wife were desperate, he said, and if they were refused the extension they would have to sell the business that represented their life savings, and move.

"We've lost our son," he said. "My wife has lost her career. If we lose our business we might just as well give up."

Times and Chronicle, **19 Sept 1991**

There was further comment in the same newspaper.

Only those with the hardest of hearts can fail to have been moved by the plight of the Mintern family of Snaith in their courageous efforts to provide the best upbringing for their paralysed and brain-damaged son Matthew.

The family's appeal to be allowed to build a ground-floor extension to accommodate their 17-year-old son, on land they already own, has been publicized in this and other newspapers, as well as on radio and television.

To support their contention that Snaith people are, in fact, more concerned about the welfare of Matthew Mintern than the loss of just 4 parking spaces, the couple handed to the council on Monday a petition signed by 1520 local people calling for a reconsideration of the compulsory purchase order.

The Minterns have an overwhelming need for sympathetic and humane consideration. Is it too much to ask Boothferry councillors to listen to them?

The petition, the media coverage and Matty in his wheelchair failed to move the council. The appeal was turned down. We turned to our MP, David Davies, who took up the case.

HUMANITARIAN DECISION ON
PARENTS' PLEA

Parents fighting for permission to build a special home extension to care for their brain-damaged son have won a major battle against their local council.

And the couple at the centre of the row have praised more than 1500 people who signed a petition in their support.

Mr and Mrs Mintern said they were certain that the weight of public opinion had influenced a Government decision in their favour. The Secretary of State for the Environment, Mr Michael Heseltine, has decided not to allow Boothferry Borough Council to use compulsory purchase powers to buy a small patch of land at the rear of the couple's pub at Snaith.

Mr and Mrs Mintern had earmarked the site to build a ground-floor extension in which to look after their 17-year-old son, who was critically injured in a road accident.

An independent inspector suggested that Boothferry's compulsory purchase order should be confirmed.

But Mr Heseltine overturned the recommendation.

He said he had reached the decision on 'humanitarian' grounds to override the planning merits of the order.

Hull Daily Mail, 2 Oct 1991

Finally we could go ahead. The council were quick to pass the plans for the bungalow extension after this, and work started early in 1992. It felt like a triumph of sorts because the alternative had been so dreadful, but none of us felt celebratory. Time and again, as we tried to cope with the transformation of Matty, we also had to cope with all this other stuff that went with it. I could never understand how people could have so little compassion towards him and us.

In April I finally passed my driving test – on my fourth attempt. I bought a silver Toyota Starlet for £500 with money I'd saved from my bar wages, which our customers called the Silver Bullet, and as the bungalow was being built I would reverse it into a pile of bricks on a fairly regular basis.

I spent most of my free time hanging around with our customers. I played in the dominoes team on Tuesday nights, the ladies' darts team on Wednesdays, and in the mixed darts league on Monday nights, where I was often the only woman on either side who got a game. Thursdays was men's darts night, and we had two teams. My dad played with the A team and I'd usually go along with the B team. Dad would give me money so that I could fulfil the land-lordly duty of getting the first round in. It felt good to pitch up at a pub in one of the neighbouring villages and head straight to the bar in front of eight men.

———

By summer, the extension was finished. Mum, Dad and Matty had a big bedroom to share, with an enormous bathroom to accommodate Matty's shower trolley. All the doors were wide enough for him to be wheeled around in the hoist, and we set up a team of carers and had regular visits from a physiotherapist. There wasn't a room for me in the bungalow, but I moved into Matty's bedroom above the pub, which was nearest to it. I liked being in Matty's room; it made me feel close to him. I mingled my possessions with his, wore his clothes and cut his jeans, several inches too long for me, into denim shorts. It was odd being both next to but separated from my family, literally under a different roof. Lots of my friends were envious of my freedom and would sometimes exclaim about how lucky I was, before remembering what was at the root of having all this space at my disposal.

All I had to do to rejoin the family was walk down the back stairs and through a communicating door we'd put in. This took me straight from the back kitchen of the pub into the big bedroom. Mum had a small office area in the corner of the room so she could do all the cashing-up and paperwork and keep an eye on Matty at the same time. We got a new safe, and the one built into the wall upstairs was no longer used. I had a few nightmares that burglars would break in and threaten to burn the place down if I wouldn't give them the code, not believing that the safe was empty. Outside we had a little paved area and a small garden, which meant we could wheel Matty out to sit in the sun without anyone seeing. It made me think of the poem 'Futility' by Wilfred Owen:

Move him into the sun – Gently its touch
*   awoke him once,*
At home, whispering of fields unsown.
Always it woke him, even in France,
Until this morning and this snow.
If anything might rouse him now
The kind old sun will know.

Think how it wakes the seeds, –
Woke, once, the clays of a cold star.
Are limbs, so dear-achieved, are sides,
Full-nerved – still warm – too hard to stir?
Was it for this the clay grew tall?
– O what made fatuous sunbeams toil
To break earth's sleep at all?

As time passed, fewer and fewer people asked about Matty because they knew there would be no progress to report. Within the pub everything was OK because we were the pub people and could get on with serving the drinks. It was outside the protection of our walls, when people saw us as individuals, that we became tainted. My dad said people would cross the road to avoid feeling that they had to ask him for news. I worked Saturday nights in the pub and before my shift would often go to buy cigarettes in the shop across the road, where I'd run into people who had been drinking away all afternoon.

'How's your kid?' they'd say. 'I don't like to ask your mum and dad.'

I couldn't work this out, the bit about not liking to ask

my parents. Did they think I didn't matter; that I was less upset than they were? Maybe it was simply that their inhibitions were loosened enough to ask. They'd had a few pints, they were picking up fags or lottery tickets on the way home to their families and woozily decided to do the decent thing and ask the question.

I can remember how much I hated that question, but I can't remember how I answered it. How many ways can you say that there has been no change? How many ways can you say that there is no news?

I still sat with Matty every day. I cuddled him and talked to him, though I'd run through all of our memories a million times and didn't have anything new to say. I brushed his hair gently over his scars. I squeezed the blackheads on his nose because I knew he'd have hated them. I'd inherited our father's acne-prone skin and Matty, like our mother, had hardly had a spot in his life until the accident. Now he was covered in them.

Once I was gently easing out the blackheads with a tissue and then wiping his nose with an Oxy pad when a single tear ran down his cheek. We never knew whether his occasional tears – never very many – had any kind of emotional backdrop or not. I wondered if the Oxy pad had made his eye water. Either way, I was distressed to think I'd hurt him. The old Matty would have hated the thought of blackheads, but probably wouldn't have liked me squeezing them either. Did this new Matty care? Didn't he have more to worry about than a few blackheads on his nose? I couldn't unravel all this in my head, couldn't work out what version of him might have wanted what at what time, but I never did it again.

Often I'd look deep into his eyes, looking for awareness. Sometimes, but I was never sure if I'd imagined it, I thought I saw a fleeting grimace, a flash of his old self realizing where and who he was. I wondered where his essence was, his soul.

THE NUT HOUSE

Somehow I got decent grades at A level and applied to the five nearest universities to study French and English. I didn't have much enthusiasm for it, but I could just about remember that this was what my pre-accident self had wanted to do. When the offers came in, I decided on Leeds. The university was just up the road from the infirmary. I wanted to stay at home, but my parents encouraged me to get a room in halls. They would visit me once a week, they promised, and I could come home at weekends.

I didn't know I was common until I went to university. I'd grown up being teased for having a posh voice and being too clever for my own good and had got used to being feted, spoiled and treated like an heiress in the pub, so it came as a bit of a shock.

I learned that 'Where did you go to school?' was not a question about geography but an attempt to pin me down and categorize me. When my new best friend Sophie introduced me to some of her other friends, they treated me like a curious pet.

'Isn't she well spoken,' one of them drawled at another, 'for someone who went to a comprehensive?'

I didn't mind any of this and thought it was quite funny.

I'd read lots of books – from *Anne of the Island* to Philip Larkin's *Jill* to *Brideshead Revisited* – about going to university and meeting other, posher, people, so I felt well prepared. I knew from books that the worst thing was to pretend to be other than you are, so I never wasted time on lying or being ashamed about my background, which I saw some students do. I was still bemused that some people seemed to genuinely think they were better than others due to birth or going to particular schools.

Sophie was the first person I met when I arrived at Lupton Flats, a university block in Headingley where, the gossip went, the Yorkshire Ripper had found one of his victims. She had brought six green wine glasses, given to her by her mother. I had never seen coloured glass before and found the notion of being given wine glasses by a parent incredibly glamorous. She'd spent the summer Interrailing, had played lacrosse on the beach in Portugal and then used her lacrosse stick to steal bread from the open-topped van parked behind tall gates at the bakery. She had her own backgammon set, her father was a surgeon, she'd been to boarding school. She was like someone out of a book and I drank her in.

On one of the very first nights I told her about Matty and she took it in her stride. Her mum had had a stroke years ago when Sophie was fourteen and had difficulties with walking and speaking. Sophie knew what it felt like to be apart from everyone else. We'd stay up all night drinking, chatting, playing Scrabble, smoking. I graduated from the Embassy or Regal I'd grown up with to Marlboro Lights, with their classy white and gold packets, and I started saying lunch instead of dinner, and dinner instead of tea.

I liked spending time with Sophie and her family, who always took me out with them when they came to visit. Her father had subscribed her to all sorts of interesting magazines, so I got used to reading *Private Eye* and the *Spectator*, and he sent us lots of the gifts given to him by grateful patients. I discovered a taste for smoked salmon and Parma ham, neither of which I'd ever eaten before.

My favourite places on campus were the Brotherton Library and the stationery shop. I bought lots of disposable fountain pens and wrote all my essays in purple ink. Sophie and I bought some silver spray paint and she stencilled stars onto our Doc Martens, hers were black, mine were green.

I didn't know how to describe myself to the new people I met. In our village I was used to being the sister of Coma Boy, the girl from the Bell and Crown, Forearms' daughter. Everyone knew everything about us. Now, out in the wider world, faced with questions from fellow students and their parents about how I'd spent my gap year, I tied myself in knots. I felt like I came from a different planet from all these innocent, undamaged people.

I tried a variety of answers to the question about whether I had any brothers and sisters:

What to say 'I have a brother.'
Pros It's truthful.
Cons They will ask a follow up, like 'What does he do?', to which 'Not much, really' is not an appropriate

response. (It is a bit funny, though, isn't it? If you really want to see it?)

Conclusion Not worth it. You'll have to explain in the end.

What to say 'No.'

Pros It's short. It doesn't bring down the mood.

Cons It's a lie. It will make you feel really bad in a biblical 'denying your God' sort of way.

Conclusion Not worth it. You'll feel rotten and, if you get to know the person better, the lie will sit poisonously between you until you have to 'fess up. Sometime someone will say 'I thought you had the air of an only child about you', and you will have no idea what to do or how to continue the conversation.

What to say 'I have a brother. He's in a permanent vegetative state after being knocked down by a car.'

Pros It's truthful.

Cons Too much. Too depressing. Doesn't even stop the conversation as people will want to ask questions about PVS. They will also want to know the prognosis. You will give answers that range from optimistically deluded to numbly unsure to misanthropically resigned. No one will know how to cope with you.

Conclusion Avoid.

What to say 'I have a brother but he's poorly after an
   accident.'
Pros It's truthful. Gives the questioner enough
   information to know the landscape without making
   everyone too sad, and allows them to say 'I'm sorry
   to hear that' and then move on to another subject.
Cons They might ask more but that's up to them.
Conclusion Best course of action.

There was the considerable problem that no one knew
what PVS meant, and it was difficult to explain. If I said
coma, people would think of a not-unpleasant Sleeping
Beauty state from which it's possible to wake up fully at any
time. 'Vegetative' was the key word, but a horrible word,
with the hideous 'cabbage', a word I never used, lurking in
the background.

If I was talking to a grown-up rather than a fellow student, once I'd negotiated all this territory and finally choked
out some version of the truth to whoever was asking, they'd
usually say, 'Your poor parents.' I used to ponder this. Now
I realize that person will have been a parent. What they were
actually thinking was, 'Thank God that didn't happen to my
child.'

Most weekends I went back to the pub, often with
Sophie. I 'introduced' her to Matty and she sat and held
his hand. I thought how different things would be if she
was meeting him as he used to be, imagined the jokes, the
laughter, all of us going out for a drink together.

We would work behind the bar, and the customers loved

Sophie and how posh she was. When a football match was on the telly and a customer asked Sophie what the half-time score was, she replied, glancing up at the screen, 'Two Love,' to everyone's great amusement. They had never seen anyone quite like her, certainly not pulling them pints.

Another Christmas came and went, our fourth in the pub.

1993 got off to a slow, cold start.

One evening we were watching the news on telly in the bungalow. A young man called Tony Bland was in a coma after being crushed in the Hillsborough disaster four years before, and his doctors, with the support of his parents, were bringing a case that he should be allowed to die by withdrawing artificial nutrition and hydration. The basic argument was that feeding someone through a tube should be considered medical treatment, just like giving antibiotics, or resuscitating someone after a heart attack. This meant that in certain cases the courts could decide that this particular medical treatment should not be given.

We'd been aware of this case but had never thought of it as having anything to do with us. We'd assumed Tony Bland was in a full coma, without periods of sleep and wake. But this report had footage of him and he looked just like Matty; it could have been a film of Matty. He was about the same age, with dark hair, wrists bent over with spasticity, the same kind of tube hanging from his nostril. He was in a hospital room and there were photos of him around his bed, just like the photos of the pre-accident Matty we had put everywhere. We looked from the boy on the screen to the boy on our sofa and the resemblance was undeni-able. The only difference was that Tony looked as if he had a bit more awareness than Matty – his eyes moved around a bit more.

In the past when Matty had had a big fit or when he had been readmitted to hospital with an infection, we had been asked by medical staff whether we wanted him treated. We had always said yes, without hesitation. Our customers were always bringing in clippings of stories in the press like 'Man wakes up from coma after 10 years', and we still believed it could happen for us. Anyway we loved Matty, regardless of his progress. We didn't want him to die.

And so we became experts at shutting out what we didn't want to hear, ignoring any evidence that indicated there was no hope.

A doctor's report from the previous July had said:

There has not been any significant improvement in his unconscious vegetative state since the injury, except that his eyes are now open.

His condition is unlikely to alter one year after injury.

'*Unlikely*,' we said then. 'Not *impossible*.'

We had always refused to accept there was no hope. We felt Matty was special; he was worth fighting for. If any man was going to wake up from a coma after years, it was this one.

But the news story and the image of poor Tony Bland, another bright, lovely boy who liked football, stayed with me. I didn't want to think about it, but I couldn't escape the knowledge that some people thought it was better for Tony not to be alive. What did that mean for Matty?

As the year went on, I got sadder and sadder. I went to some of my classes, but the French terrified me. I'd become mute. I could hardly speak in my own language unless I was medicated with alcohol, so it was a torture to try to express myself in another. English classes were a bit better, though the lecture rooms we had to go to for Shakespeare made me feel claustrophobic.

I had a tutor for Critical Practices I liked. He waved my essay on Russian Formalism at me, and said, 'This is exceptional. You can really write. I've been showing it round the department.' I felt a flicker of enjoyment, a memory of how good it felt to enthuse a teacher, but it disappeared.

At the end of the year, in my final tutorial with him, he looked at me rather sadly and said, 'I don't think you ever really surpassed the high point of Russian Formalism.'

I no longer had any interest in achieving things. Once, I had cared. I could still remember my despair when I got 93% to Kelvyn Prescott's 94% in our English exam at school – I had been able to accept that he was better than me at Maths, but I had thought of English as my territory – but now that grit, determination, even interest was gone. I was simply finding a way to crawl through time rather than caring about what I did with it.

I went home a bit less and stayed in Leeds more, hardly leaving my student flat. I slept all day and then stayed up all night, drinking and playing cards or Scrabble with Sophie until she went to bed, and then drinking and reading on my own. I cried myself to sleep most mornings to the backdrop of birdsong and the first light coming through my curtains.

Mum realized everything had gone haywire with me and she suggested I go away for a few days. She picked me up and drove me to a retreat in North Leeds that had been recommended to her. She had brought me everything she thought I might need for the duration, including cigarettes. She sat on my bed with me and held my hand.

'I wonder if I could have another child?' she said. 'It might not be too late. Would that make things better for you?'

I was overwhelmed by her love for me, but I didn't want another sibling. I wanted the one I'd lost. I couldn't see how a baby would measure up to the vast hole left by the pre-accident version of Matty.

The retreat was OK. There was a library, where I read lots of P. G. Wodehouse, and I found it a relief to not have to put on an act, to be surrounded by people who knew how sad I was.

After a few days Mum picked me up and took me back to Lupton Flats. She'd tidied my room, changed the bedding, washed up all the dirty crockery. It was no longer a den of squalor. She also arranged for me to see a therapist called Jane once a week.

The first time I went to see Jane I took a cartoon I'd torn out of the *Spectator*. It showed a man on a couch and the speech bubble said something like, 'I had a wonderful childhood. It's being grown-up that I can't handle.'

I didn't tell many people about the therapy, and if I did, I called it 'going to the nuthouse', but I liked Jane. I liked the

Klimt print on her wall, the boxes of tissues dotted around her room. I liked the couch, though I never lay on it. Jane definitely did me some good. We talked about the idea of Matty One and Matty Two, how I couldn't connect what he was now to what he had been, and how it felt disloyal to the Matty who was left to grieve for the Matty that we'd lost. We worked out during those sessions that I finally knew that he wasn't going to get better and that I needed to concentrate on accepting the situation as it was.

Mum didn't have another baby, though they did get another dog, deciding on a pure-bred Labrador who would have a gentle temperament around Matty. They chose him from a kennels in Leeds, where his name was 'Midnight Galaxy'. We called him Murphy after the Irish stout that was a big seller in the pub. He was no replacement for Polly, but we grew to love him and he encouraged us to go out for long walks along the riverbank. We'd walk for miles, along farm-land with grazing cattle, watching the herons landing and fishing. Murphy was never a dog to chase a stick on dry land, but he came into his own in the water. He would watch the stick being thrown into the fast flowing river, work out the trajectory, and set out on a course to intercept it. He was an astonishingly dim dog, and apart from this one trick, he only ever showed intelligence about the pursuit of food.

I carried on seeing Jane all the way through my second year and became a bit less insular. She diagnosed Post Traumatic Stress Disorder and said she thought that all my difficulties were a direct result of what had happened to Matty. She didn't think I was mad.

I could see that it was better to be crying soberly at Jane than to be crying all over anyone who would listen when I was drunk, and I realized that I could contain the extremes of my sadness within the fifty minutes I spent sitting in her armchair or, sometimes, on the beanbag on the floor. I tried to behave more like a normal person when I was out in the world, and it worked. I became cheerful, even boisterous. No one had the least idea how I felt on the inside.

On my twenty-first birthday, the card my parents gave me had a large cheque and an advert for a Renault Clio tucked inside it. We all liked the TV adverts with Nicole and Papa. I chose a purple one, and not only did all our customers call me Nicole for a while, but I started calling my dad Papa; and it stuck. It became a long-standing joke whenever we were serving together. It was the first time we'd managed to feel a little bit positive about anyone's birthday since the accident.

A drunk customer, congratulating me on being lucky enough to have a brand new car, said, 'Of course, it will all come to you now,' waving his hands around at the pub. Another told me that my dad must be making too much money out of them if he could afford a new car for me. It wasn't unusual for people to say this sort of thing. The downside of having the pub was that people were obsessively interested in us and could swing quickly between fondness and resentment. If we got a new carpet for the bar, half our customers would say 'nice carpet', and the other half would say we should put the price of the beer down instead of wasting money on furnishings. I was used to people speculating over my boyfriends and my future, and this wasn't the first time that someone had made the link between Matty's accident and my eventual financial benefit. I never knew what to say. Could these people know me so little that they'd think I'd be able to see it as some kind of silver lining? Now that I was spending time with people who weren't from Yorkshire, I realized it was a peculiarly Yorkshire trait to take pride in being unpleasant and intrusive. 'I speak as I find,' people would say imperiously at the bar after causing someone great offence.

I was getting a bit fed up with the lack of privacy, with everyone knowing everything about us.

Once, when I was behind the bar, someone said, 'I saw your dad in the doctor's this morning. What's up with him?'

'I don't know,' I said, 'I didn't know he was there. Should I go and ask him so I can come back and put you in the picture?'

Matty's birthday came round a month after mine. We had always tried to have some sort of a celebration, but three and a half years after the accident it was becoming increasingly difficult. Presents were impossible. If there was anything at all that we thought might improve his life, we wouldn't wait for his birthday to hand it over. I usually gave him a CD. I'd wrap it up, put it into the hand that wasn't twisted up with spasticity, move his fingers over the wrapping paper and open it with him.

Three days after his birthday, Matty was admitted to Killingbeck Hospital. His lungs were full of fluid, and despite the strongest antibiotics his condition had deteriorated. The inside of his mouth was coated with a sort of scabbing, and when we tried to ease it off with a sponge stick it left raw flesh beneath. We pointed this out to a nurse. 'Well, he is very poorly,' she said, clearly thinking there were bigger things to worry about.

We drove to the hospital and back every day through labyrinthine roadworks, washed and cared for Matty as usual, and watched as the medical staff suctioned the yellowy green slime off his lungs. Once, to give ourselves a change from the hospital canteen, Mum and I went out for a walk in the freezing February air and had lunch at a pub down the road. I ate half a plate of liver and onions and then went to the loo and threw it all up. I looked at myself in the mirror and rested my hot forehead against it and closed my eyes. How could it just keep getting worse? How much more could I bear? I felt trapped in a never-ending narrative of awfulness.

There was talk of an operation – they wanted to drill a hole into one of Matty's lungs to relieve the fluid inside, pretty much the same as they'd done at Pontefract Hospital two years previously; he still had the scar. Matty was last on the list for theatre that day because they didn't want his infection to harm others using the operating table, and as we waited in his small room for the porters to take him down, he started to let out a soft moaning sound, which increased in volume until it was audible throughout the ward. Suddenly a spurt of foul-smelling thick yellow pus burst out from the old scar and splashed all over the sheets. I had the taste of sick in my mouth but choked back the urge to vomit. The operation was cancelled; the doctors had their hole. They pumped in antibiotics and put a drain in so that the rest of the filthy sludge could be removed, and we could look forward to returning him home again.

After three weeks in Killingbeck, Matty came home with a tube coming out of his side and a bag to collect the pus from his lung. The homecoming was subdued. Every other time he'd come close to death and then survived we'd treated it as a triumph. This was the first time I caught myself wondering if it might have been better if he'd died. Would Matty have wanted this life? Unable to do anything except open his eyes, have epileptic fits, occasionally make noises when in pain? I didn't allow these thoughts to develop, nor did I see how I could ever voice them to my parents, but they were there.

I became obsessed with what would happen if Matty died, as neither of us had been baptized, and I had read novels where the unbaptized weren't allowed to be buried in church grounds. I didn't dare ask anyone about this, so instead announced that I'd decided I wanted to be baptized and thought Matty should be too. My parents went along with it, though they probably thought it was deranged, and I went to see our local vicar, who arranged it all. It was a hot summer's day when we went to the church, but cold when we stepped inside. I hoped to feel something – I wanted to be moved by God; I thought that life looked like it was a whole lot easier if you had religious belief. But I wasn't touched in any way I noticed, and Matty made no response to having holy water splashed on his face, though I hadn't expected he would. Still, I'd achieved my aim. If he died now, he could be buried in our local church if we wanted.

The time came for me to go away to France for a year as part of my degree. I didn't want to leave home and be so far away from my family, and had various conversations with my parents about whether I could change my major to English and not go, but I was too numbly lethargic to do much about it and couldn't summon up the energy to ask the necessary questions. I hadn't done any of the various things you had to do to be a teaching assistant, so I ended up taking the option that seemed the least effort and going to a language school in Caen.

I drove down to Portsmouth and took the midnight ferry to Caen. Jane had suggested I try to write things down, so I bought a notebook with a picture of the Eiffel Tower on it from the ferry shop and sat in the bar staring at it and drinking mini bottles of red wine. I couldn't find any words. I wrote down the names of the French authors I was studying: Molière, Racine, Sartre, Camus, Appolinaire, Simone de Beauvoir. The purple ink looked pleasing against the white page. All those dead French men and one woman. I couldn't manage anything else.

I spent my first night in France in a tiny hotel in Caen. I chose my meal from the *prix fixe* menu: a steak that came with salsify – a yellowish vegetable that I'd never seen before – and a half carafe of red wine. I ate slowly, drank quickly and thought how Matty would never eat a meal alone in a French restaurant like this. This led me to wondering what we'd all be doing now if the accident had never happened, if I'd made him get that lift home with me, if he was still undamaged. I couldn't visualize the person I'd be now. Was there a parallel-universe version of me uncrippled by pain and love and able simply to enjoy the consumption of unfamiliar vegetables and experiences?

I found somewhere to rent in Courseulles-sur-Mer, a small seaside town built around one of the D-Day landing beaches that had been taken by the Canadian forces, where many of the streets referenced the war: rue du 6 Juin, avenue de la Combattante, avenue de la Libération. My little studio flat was in a three-storey apartment block on rue des Canadiens – one room with a sofabed, a tiny balcony, a *coin cuisine* with two hob rings, a sink and a fridge, and a bathroom with a three-quarter-size bath and a bidet that I used to wash my underwear in because I was scared of the launderette. Rubbish went down a *vide-ordure*, a little chute out in the passageway. Once, drunk, I threw my door keys down it by mistake and had to go and forage in the basement, where I found them perched on the top of everyone else's refuse. My favourite thing was the pigeonhole postboxes at the entrance of the building. I felt a frisson of grown-up enjoyment as I filled my name in on my own little box.

An interesting mishmash of people of all nationalities congregated at the language school. Our teacher was a tiny, dapper chap who carried a little handbag and liked talking about Dickens, particularly Marteen Choozleveet. After class, we'd sit in the canteen playing cards and drinking fiercely strong coffee that came out of a machine and only cost two francs. We all spoke mainly French to each other, as it was the language we had in common, and I felt a flicker of pleasure that I was playing cards in French with German,

Japanese and Russian friends. We asked each other questions about our lives, but I couldn't bring myself to try to explain Matty's situation in French – I could hardly manage it in English. So I learned how to claim I was an only child and lied in response to the brothers or sisters question: '*Je suis fille unique.*'

Most of us were students, but some were partners of French people trying to brush up their language skills.

'That's the thing about France,' said one of our American classmates, picking at her lunch. 'You fall in love with a guy and follow him home, and then you find out that his countrymen plaster goddamn mayonnaise all over every single little thing they make you eat.'

There was one English guy who could hardly speak French at all who told us that his French girlfriend didn't know any English.

'It's not just sexual, though,' he said.

'Hmm,' said one of the other English students as he walked off. 'Perhaps they play a lot of chess.'

I was drawn to a Welsh girl called Rhian. She wore floaty clothes and long scarves and enormous dark eyes shone out of her pale face. She was a Baptist and didn't drink. There was another Baptist among us who went on and on about being 'in the front line for God', and kept saying 'rock on for Jesus'. She had a French boyfriend, also a Baptist, who she'd met through church, and she talked a lot about how much she wanted to have sex with him and how they were both being tempted. He came to see her once and she proudly introduced him to everyone. He was tall and thin with an enormous nose and it was difficult not to imagine them resisting temptation together.

On my way home in the evenings I'd call into Champion, the large supermarket on the outskirts of Courseulles. There were wonderful things there. Lobsters lurked in massive tanks, and ready-made hors d'oeuvres were laid out in beautifully regimented lines behind counters. I'd look at them for a while: tiny asparagus tips perched on crab mousse, blinis with smoked salmon and a smattering of caviar. Sometimes I'd imagine what they'd taste like, but I never bought anything. They seemed a bit grand. Always I'd turn away from what seemed like another world and go instead to buy bread, cheese and tomatoes. This, to me, was still a feast, the baguettes crispy on the outside and soft on the inside. I bought Camembert, Brie and a pungent square called Pont-l'Évêque. I loved the sumptuous redness of the tomatoes, nothing like the watery orange balls that were sliced up and plonked next to the cress in an English salad. And then booze, of course. I filled my trolley with booze. I'd have a couple of beers as I ate and then open a bottle of red wine. Most nights I opened a second.

I spent a lot of time in Second World War cemeteries and in the war museum in Caen, which was called *Un Musée pour la Paix*. I worked in the library there on my dissertation about the French Resistance, pondering whether I'd be better able to cope with Matty's situation if we were living during a war, when death and disablement were more commonplace. If he were shot in front of me as we were embarked on some clandestine activity for the Resistance, would I throw myself on his body and wait for my own bullet or would I fade into the crowd, wanting to survive? I met an Auschwitz survivor in the library, a lovely man who took an interest in my studies and liked to talk to me in English about his experiences. He told me he was born in Lithuania and had been deported to Auschwitz from France, where he was working as a decorator. He credited his survival to being able to pick up languages very quickly, which meant he could joke with the camp guards.

I dreamt about Matty a lot. Sometimes he was better, but with some kind of modification – he was very little, or only had one leg. I spent these dreams reassuring him that everything would be OK. Other times he'd be in sepia, like the young Jewish men in the photos I was looking at in the library. I needed to warn him of an approaching danger, but he wouldn't listen.

At weekends I'd pick Rhian up from the church family she was staying with and we'd go sightseeing. When we stood on the ramparts of Mont Saint-Michel, I remembered being there with Matty on a school French exchange trip where I'd drunk too much vodka, and Matty had been upset and his crying face was the last thing I'd seen before I passed out. It felt like a million years ago. I could hardly grasp that Matty had once cried over me as I now cried over him.

From a high tower we looked down towards the rocks below, and I wondered if lovelorn medieval monks had ever thrown themselves off.

After our days out, I'd drop Rhian off then go home via the supermarket and drink till I was off my face. I couldn't stand being alone with thoughts of my poor, broken brother. I couldn't turn off the light. I'd drink until I dropped, or read until I fell asleep with the book still in my hand. I clutched books to me like a child with a comfort blanket. I'd wake in the night on the sofa – I rarely bothered to pull it out into a bed – and listen to the World Service while smoking. I was so sad, and I didn't know if I was sad simply because of what had happened to Matty or because I was mad.

After three lonely months of sending letters home to be read aloud to Matty about what a great time I was having, it was Christmas and I could go back. Rhian accompanied me as far as the service station on my route that wasn't too far for her dad to come and pick her up from. She wasn't going to come back to France but was instead heading on to Russia for the rest of the year. I was going to miss her. She gave me a box of pastels and a drawing pad as a parting gift.

Up the M1, then towards the North. The first sign that I was nearly home was the plumes of smoke from the power stations that surrounded us: Drax, Ferrybridge, Eggborough.

It was getting dark by the time I turned off the motorway and drove down the winding road towards Snaith. I passed the Rainbow, passed the scene of Matty's accident, his old school, into the village, past the church and the library. I was suddenly nervous and drove around the block a couple of times, looking at the Christmas lights on the houses and pubs.

I pulled into our car park and braced myself against the Yorkshire cold as I got my stuff out of the boot. I'd bought gifts for everyone who worked in the pub or with Matty.

Wine, calavados, jars of *tripes à la mode de Caen* to give to our Saturday afternoon back-room customers who often prepared snacks to sustain them through a long afternoon of watching the racing and liked something disgusting called chitterlings. The fruit tarts had a dishevelled look and the Camemberts were giving off a bit of a whiff after their long drive.

As I walked into the bungalow, Matty was propped in a seated position on the sofa, pillows under his spastic arm, and one of the people who looked after him was massaging his feet. There was something biblical about it, and I realized in that moment that we'd constructed a crazy world around a wounded messiah. I didn't think it should go on. I didn't think Matty should go on.

I thought, '*He is fucked and this is fucked-up.*'

I sat next to Matty and looked into his eyes, their awful blankness. There was no sparkle, no sign that anything was going on. I held his hand and told him bright and cheerful lies about France, but I knew there was no longer any point in talking to him. He was gone. I now felt more sure than ever before that it would have been better for him, better for everyone, if he'd died on the night of the accident.

CHEER UP, LOVE

It was a grim Christmas. I held my new certainty to myself like a shameful secret. The high point was when I won £50 playing a domino game called 'Barmy' on Boxing Day. The low point was when I was talking to Mum while she was showering Matty in his trolley and noticed that he had a slight erection. I'd seen this before; we used to think of it as a positive sign that something was happening in his brain. Now, remembering the time when Matty went with his girlfriend to the doctor's to get the morning-after pill when they'd had a condom failure, it seemed utterly tragic that his wrecked body could still register a flicker of residual sexual interest. That night I dreamt that my parents died and that it became my responsibility to look after Matty. In the dream, I couldn't get the hoist to work and dropped him on the bathroom floor.

I set off back to France on 7 January, taking the midnight ferry and waking up on a recliner seat on the morning of my twenty-second birthday. I drove to Courseulles along the coast road with 'The Body of an American' by the Pogues playing on repeat, to find that my little flat was freezing and there were no letters in my postbox. I opened the birthday present my parents had sent me off with. Two jumpers: one blue, one brown. I wondered if I should try to do something, and then realized that, now Rhian had left, I didn't have a single number for anyone in France. I thought about taking myself out for a meal in one of the restaurants along the seafront.

There was no hot water, but I felt filthy after sleeping in my clothes on the ferry and decided to make a bath by boiling pans of water, but it took too long and when I spilt a bit over my hand I gave up. After running my hand under the cold tap for a few minutes, I put the World Service on and cuddled up under my duvet with a bottle of red wine, smoking and reading. I was stuck into a trilogy of books called *La Bicyclette bleue,* essentially a *Gone With the Wind*-style storyline set on a French vineyard during the Second World War, and I read them again and again.

I limped through January and February, only going to some of my classes. I'd spend hours dithering about whether or not to leave the flat, but was only ever really motivated out of it by the need to buy more booze. I'd grown to hate this time of year, which was cold, and then had first Christmas, then my birthday and then Matty's to get through. I hated the way that the accident had made times that should have been joyous even worse than normal days. I couldn't bring myself to phone home on Matty's twenty-first birthday and go through the charade of the phone being held to his ear so that I could talk to him. I did send him a picture: a drawing I'd done with Rhian's pastels of the view over the rooftops from my little balcony. It wasn't very good.

I began to find words. I bought orange Rhodia note-books with squared paper and scribbled away in purple ink. I wrote down observations about France and started writing a novel. The heroine was a bit like me but much thinner and prettier with silvery blonde hair. Her twin brother was in PVS and she was trying to work out how to live on without him. She was called Ursula and he was called Danny, which were names my parents had considered giving to us – Ursula because Mum was reading *Women in Love* when she got pregnant, Danny because Dad liked the song 'Danny Boy'. I don't know why I made them twins. Perhaps I wanted to feel as though I'd once shared a womb with Matty, not just the back seat of the car.

On St Patrick's Day night I phoned home. Dad was making Irish stew for the whole pub and the band had just arrived. I longed to be there, surrounded by warmth and noise, drawing shamrocks, love hearts and people's initials into the creamy foam heads of the pints of Guinness. My answer was to go to Champion, buy a bottle of whisky and drink it all, playing the Pogues and chain-smoking Gauloises.

The weather got warmer. One evening, I was loading my shopping into the boot in the Champion car park when some English boys saw my number plates and ran over to chat. I was more than ready to be befriended. They were posh and boisterous and one of them, Charlie, lived round the corner. The other two were both called Simon, Tall Si and Small Si, though even Small Si was over six feet. They made me laugh. I drank beer with them, giggled at their girlfriend stories, played Frisbee on the beach. *Me!* I thought. *Me playing Frisbee on the beach!* I hung around with them in town, sitting on the grass at the place de la République or drinking beer in the bars and then staying over at the Simons' flat. They made up endless variations of 'She was only the landlord's daughter but she lay on the bar and said pump'.

Charlie and I drove in and out of town together a lot, listening to the radio which played a mix of French and English music. We liked a singer called Francis Cabrel, and were amused by a rap song half in English, half in French that included the line, 'Life's a bitch and then you die, *voilà.*' The most played song was 'A Girl Like You' by Edwyn Collins.

I liked Charlie and liked driving around with him in his red Golf. I'd told him about Matty the first time we'd got drunk together, and he'd held me as I cried. One of the towns nearby was called Matthieu, and as we drove by it one sunny day, Charlie told me that a friend called Matt was planning to pinch a road sign to take home. I was eating cherries and spitting the stones out of the window.

'We could get one for you,' he said, smiling sideways at me. 'You could take one home for your brother.'

I was moved by this suggestion. Charlie was exactly the sort of person Matty would have been friends with, which made me wish Matty were here to play Frisbee on the beach, spit cherry stones out of car windows and steal his own road sign.

It was the fiftieth anniversary of D-Day and there were celebrations everywhere. All the cafes had signs that said

'Welcome to our liberators', though none of the people working in them looked either welcoming or grateful. It was bittersweet witnessing elderly Americans trying to bond with apathetic waiters by describing their wartime experiences in loud English.

One Saturday near the end of our time in France, after we'd all spent the day on the beach drinking, I agreed to go bungee jumping with the boys, never really thinking I'd go through with it.

They came to pick me up the next morning. I heard beeping from the car park and looked down to see Charlie hanging out of the car window.

'Come on! Time to go jump off a bridge!'

Tall Si was in the passenger seat, so I got into the back with Small Si.

Charlie drove all the way there, while the boys kept saying that I'd have to tuck my T-shirt in and told stories of girls showing off their breasts as they hung upside down.

We arrived at the Viaduc de la Soulevre and it was beautiful: a disused bridge over a valley with a river flowing below. We queued, paid and got weighed. I was embarrassed when they wrote our weight on our hands – 69 kilos for me. I wouldn't mind weighing that now, but at the time I thought I was fat.

Then it was a long wait whilst we watched the other people. Some jumped out confidently into the air, some plopped reluctantly over the edge with their eyes shut. There were no girls. I saw three men get to the edge and then not be able to do it, and knew that if the old Matty were here, he'd jump with magnificent exuberance. The sun was shining and I started to feel pleased with myself, a bit adventurous, even a bit cocky. I told the boys I'd go first, and tucked my T-shirt into my jeans. The operator fixed the harness around my Doc boots and then, because I could no longer move my feet to walk, helped me shuffle out to the edge.

There was a camera at the jumping-off point. I waved at it and grinned as I charged out into the air and waited for the blissful falling.

Afterwards, as I sat on the riverbank below and watched all the boys leap, I felt completely alive. We climbed the steep steps of the valley and collected our souvenir T-shirts, put them on and sat in the bar drinking beer and watching the video footage of our jumps. I loved the way I looked, smiling and laughing into the camera. I looked free, unfettered.

We drove back to Caen via a fairground where we went on terrifying rides that almost made bungee jumping look easy, high on adrenaline. I felt like a proper young person with proper friends, and that night I phoned home.

'I went bungee jumping, Dad. It was amazing.'

'What did you do that for?' he answered, his voice in my ear, a country away. 'I've got one brain-damaged child, I don't want another.'

That brought me down to earth.

'Cheer up, love, it might never happen.'

I was in the ferry terminal at Ouistreham writing into one of my orange notebooks when a lorry driver stopped at my table to say something. I hadn't heard him.

'Sorry, what?'

'Cheer up. It might never happen.'

I stared at him. It might never happen? But it has, it did.

He made a face and moved off, and I sat shaking at the table. Didn't I have enough to contend with without putting up with that?

I tried to keep calm by sketching his face into my note-book, giving shape to his weedy moustache, his snaggled teeth. I was working away at my novel, which now had a title. It was called *The Survivors' Club*. Ursula was deciding not to go home to England after the year in France. She was looking for jobs in Europe, was going to drop out of univer-sity, had realized that she had to cut herself off from her family if she were to survive.

I wasn't doing that. I didn't want to go home, but I was still going back. I didn't want to see the Matty who was being kept alive in his own special little house; I wanted the Matty who would have been there at the bungee jumping. I'd never taken Charlie up on his offer to steal me the road sign because there didn't seem any point.

I got on the ferry and sat near a window, smoking. I felt like I was splintering into little bits. I watched the quayside in the curiously grey Normandy sunlight, and thought how my dad, if he were there, would be taking an interest in all the activity on shore, watching the men make the boat ready. I thought how terrible it was that we'd become so scared as a family. We hardly dared cross a road without waiting for the green man. All the life and joy had been shunted out of us by Matty's accident and was now being squeezed out of us by the act of keeping him alive. All of our love for him had gone wrong. Would it have been better if we'd loved him less, had worked less hard to keep him alive? He'd surely be in a better place if we'd let the doctors stop treating him years ago, if it could all be over for him.

Tears were running down my face. I didn't know how I was going to be able to talk to my parents about all this, but I knew I had to find a way.

As we set sail, I watched a man walk to the end of the pier and then turn into a pigeon and fly off.

I shook my head. *I've been reading too much about crazy French novelists*, I thought. *Either I'm having a surrealist moment, or I've gone completely mad.*

It wasn't as hard as I thought in the end. Mum looked terrible when I got home, thin and haggard. She'd had her fortieth birthday while I was away, and having always looked so pretty and young, now she was drawn and old. And Dad was piling on weight. He'd always been big and strong, but was starting to look fat. Matty, of course, was the same as always.

'Hello, old chap, *bonjour, mon vieux*,' I said.

I felt I had to put on a bit of a show for everyone else. I sat next to him for a bit, holding his hand, and as usual there was nothing, not an iota of a response. I felt a huge wave of compassion for this poor creature, this shell of a person. I couldn't believe that anyone would want to live like this – though at least, I thought, he didn't know that he lived like this. This thing, this entity, bore no relation to our Matty. I looked into his vacant eyes. I no longer expected to see any evidence of his soul; rather I hoped that there was no soul there to suffer.

'Mum looks bloody awful,' I said to Dad when we went out for a drink together. 'I don't think she can carry on.'

'We're stuck,' said Dad. 'We don't know what to do. There isn't anything else.'

'There must be,' I said. 'Let's talk to her about it.'

The next day we all took Murphy down to the riverbank and had a long talk. We couldn't talk at home because of Matty and because of all the people who looked after him popping in and out. With the distance that being in France had given me, I could see that the bungalow was like a hospital for one person with everything revolving around Matty's care. There were notice boards with drug regimens and charts showing his temperature, pulse and respiration pinned up on them, the physio room with a tilt table, wedges and oxygen tanks. The cupboard was full of Ensure, bed linen, towels, suppositories, Epilim, convenes, bags for urine. My parents' lives were not a priority. They had little privacy – they shared a bedroom with Matty – and not much identity beyond being part of Matty's care team. Perhaps at one time, when there was a prospect of improvement, this huge subjugation of the rest of the family had felt like a good and right thing. Now it seemed perverse. It felt like the three of us were sitting on Matty's funeral pyre and refusing to get off.

'I don't think this can go on, Mum,' I said as we watched Murphy swimming for sticks.

'I know it's mad,' she said. 'I know he doesn't know where he is or who we are, but what can we do? We've seen hospital wards where no one cleans a wet or soiled bed unless visitors are expected. We can't do that to Matty, whether he's aware of it or not.'

We talked to our GP about our plight, and he arranged

a week's respite care in Goole hospital to give us time to formulate a plan.

We had been offered a hospital place at Scunthorpe or Goole on Matty's discharge from Leeds all that time ago, but now it was made clear that a permanent hospital bed was no longer on offer, so we visited various care homes in the area. But none of the staff seemed to understand that it was possible to have as non-existent a level of response as Matty did.

'Oh, you can leave him here without any worries,' said a breezy matron. 'Just let us know his signals, his yes and his no, and we can do exactly what you would do.'

If he had signals for yes and no we wouldn't be here, I thought, and we got out of there as fast as we could.

We found the ideal solution in our own village, a small care home called Snaith Hall run by a kind family who knew us and knew the story. We wanted to have our own carer come in each day to do his bath, so that we could be sure he wasn't overlooked if they were busy.

'It's not necessary,' said gentle Mr McEnroe in his soft Irish accent. 'We'll care for him well. But if it helps you to do that then we have no problem with it.'

In August, five years after the accident, Matty was moved into Snaith Hall. Sue had helped with Matty's care in the bungalow and was happy to go into the Hall every day to do his bath. Mum went to visit every Sunday and sat with him for an hour or two, reading from the papers. I went with her the first time but found it too sad to see him there. Although I knew this was the best solution, although the Hall was very pleasant, although I knew Matty wasn't aware of anything, I still felt terribly guilty at the thought of him being there alone.

When I was getting ready to go again the next Sunday, Mum asked if I was sure I wanted to.

'You don't have to, you know.'

'Then I won't,' I said.

I was grateful to be spared, and I didn't go again. Now that I thought it would be better for Matty if he died, I didn't know how to be with his physical body.

One night I was serving behind the bar when a young man asked me if I was Cathy. He said he knew my brother.

'Oh,' I said, surprised I didn't know him. 'That must have been a long time ago.'

'No,' he said. 'I'm a care assistant up at the Hall. I look after him.'

I felt a bit sick. He was smiling at me, clearly just wanting to make friends, but I felt invaded.

You'll know I don't visit him, then, I wanted to say, but didn't. *So why would you think I'd want to chat about him over the bar?*

As far as possible, I tried to put Matty out of my mind. Books helped. Booze helped. I spent the summer working in the pub, drinking hard at every opportunity. We often did lock-ins, just a few, very trusted customers at the end of the night for an extra couple of drinks. No one paid for anything; we thought of it as having people over in our own house. Mum and Dad would go to bed, and I'd stay up half the night drinking and joking. We'd turn off all the lights in the pub except the bar lights, and we'd invent drinks, setting up rounds of flaming Drambuie, seeing which spirits would go well with Guinness. I trained myself to like Campari that summer and learned how to open bottles of beer with my teeth. All I had to do was stay sober enough to lock the door and set the burglar alarm.

Britpop had arrived, and the summer unfolded to the sound of Pulp's 'Common People' playing again and again on the jukebox. My parents and I felt liberated, could take days out together without having to arrange cover for Matty, could go back to the bungalow and not be faced with his blank stare.

One sunny afternoon in late August we went to York. We had a long lunch and then Mum went off shopping while Dad and I had a drink outside the King's Head on the river-bank. We loved this pub. It had a picture of Richard III on its sign and marks inside that showed the levels the water got to every time it flooded, which it did every couple of years or so.

There was a carnival atmosphere – men with no shirts on sitting on the bridge over the river. 'They'll start jumping in as the day goes on,' Dad said. On the next table a group of Geordie lads who had lost all their money at the races were earning their fare home by eating live wasps for £1 a time. They'd trap them in an empty pint pot, get the pound, and then pop them into their mouths. There were plenty of takers, and once they'd raised enough money they strolled off to the train station.

In the middle of all the joviality, Dad and I were deep in talk. We both felt that even though life was much better for us since Matty had gone into the nursing home, it was really no better for him. Would he want to be in a home with old people, unable to speak, move, or express an opinion? Would he want his food pumped into his stomach, his dribble wiped, his pee collected in a bag, his poo controlled by suppositories? We both agreed that it would be better for him if he died. The Tony Bland case had alerted us to a legal path. No pillows over his head, no overdosing on the medication.

Mum came back from shopping and sat down next to us.

'We've been talking about Tony Bland,' I said.

Her face crumpled. 'I'm not ready,' she said. 'Let me get used to the nursing home first. I'm not ready to talk about anything else yet.'

We agreed we wouldn't bring it up again until she raised it.

As we gathered our stuff and left, I saw that the couple at the next table were staring at us. I realized that we probably sounded like we were planning a murder.

I went back to Leeds for my final year feeling less burdened than at any other time since the accident. I moved in with Sophie on Delph Lane, a nice little street just a ten-minute walk from the university. There was a wonderful curry house called Naffees just up the road, and we went there a lot. I'd order a lamb dopiaza with a paratha, eat half, and ask them to pack up the rest so I could have it for breakfast the next day.

Sophie was keen to introduce me to her friend, John. They had just spent a year in Moscow together.

'You'll really like him,' she said. 'He's just like you.'

His house had fallen through, so we invited him to stay on our sofa until he got sorted. He had lots of good stories about Russia – the huge cockroaches, how difficult it was to buy food, how he'd travelled around with a Russian MP and been taught to shoot at a firing range.

'Must have been a proper culture shock,' I said. 'Much more exciting than my few months in Normandy.'

'That's because I'm so windswept and interesting,' he said. 'I think you should fall in love with me.'

We started seeing each other, but I knew I had to tell him about Matty if I wanted him to really know me. I dithered over it for ages as I was enjoying feeling like a normal person and didn't want to introduce gloom into this exciting new relationship. But one night, after several drinks at our kitchen table, I said I needed to tell him something.

'Oh God,' he said, 'I knew you were too good to be true. You've got a "thing", haven't you?'

'What?'

'Every girl I've ever gone out with has had some shitty secret, some melodrama. Come on then, what's yours?'

I hated him in that moment. 'Just fuck off,' I said.

'No, go on. Tell me – we might as well get it over with. I've known all along you've been gagging to tell me something.'

I stared at him. I wanted him to leave.

'What is it? Did your French teacher like you a bit too much? Are you not over your parents' divorce? Did one of your best friends have sex with you and then not talk to you again?'

'OK,' I said. 'My brother was knocked down by a car when he was sixteen and I was seventeen. He's in a Persistent Vegetative State, which means he has periods of wake and sleep but nothing else. His brain is completely fucked. My dad and I want him to die and are thinking about applying to the courts, but my mum says she's not ready. That's my thing.'

I was crying now. 'I loved him. I love him. That's my thing.'

'Fuck. I'm sorry. I'm so sorry. Come here,' he said.

We got drunk and I cried all night. And from that time on, John and I were inseparable.

———

My parents adored John from the off and he settled easily into pub life, coming home with me most weekends.

We took him to a darts finals night at a working men's club in Goole which deteriorated into a fist-fight on the stage when one of the younger players mooned and the MC took exception and lamped him.

'It's another kind of culture shock, isn't it?' I said to John. His eyes were out on stalks, but he took it all in his stride.

I fared less well in his milieu. I tended to treat all grown-ups as though they were customers at the pub, which didn't suit a lot of people. I didn't know how to behave like a nice middle-class boy's girlfriend. At a dinner at Chester golf club, the man next to me asked in a very posh voice if I played golf.

'No.'

'Do you play bridge?'

'No.'

There was a long silence, which I broke by telling him I played darts.

'How very unusual,' he said, before turning to his other side for the rest of the meal.

Over the course of that last year, Mum and Dad came to Leeds a lot. Often I'd take John or Sophie with me to meet them for lunch and we'd spend the time laughing and joking.

One day, Mum suggested I come alone so that we could all talk about Matty. I went to meet them off the train and we walked to Jumbo, a Chinese restaurant in the city centre. It had no windows, and I liked the way that, in winter, we'd go in during daylight and come out a few hours later to be surprised by the dark.

'I've been thinking a lot,' Mum said. 'I'm grateful to you both for letting me have the time, and now I can see it's not right to leave Matty like that. We need to be brave and take action. It's our responsibility.'

This felt like a huge step. We discussed what to do next.

'I still can't bear the thought of it,' I said. 'I see the legal reasons why it has to be a withdrawal of treatment rather than an intervention, but it seems so cruel and uncivilized.'

We all agreed. We believed it was best for Matty to die, but still hoped that his life might end naturally. The staff at the nursing home were aware of our wishes and now wouldn't use antibiotics to treat any infection, but time marched on, and despite having several bouts of illness, Matty always survived. We were in limbo.

I graduated in the summer of 1996 and we had a party in the bungalow to celebrate. There was lots of champagne and one of the ladies from the darts team who usually only drank Diet Coke walked smack into the French windows. She wasn't hurt and everyone laughed and carried on letting their hair down.

Later on in the evening, I was sitting outside on a bench with one of my favourite customers, who was a bit of a rogue, when he said, 'You've got amazing parents. Maybe I'd have been able to make something of my life if I'd had parents like yours.'

I knew that I was lucky. I decided to try from then on

to focus on that good fortune, to count my blessings and spend less time breaking my heart over Matty. But it wasn't easy.

After graduating, I started working full time at the pub. It was supposed to be temporary – John had moved to London and I was going to join him – but I started to get ill. The doctor said I had irritable bowel syndrome. It was painful and embarrassing and, when I had a flare-up, I couldn't go anywhere as I needed to be near a toilet.

One evening there was a horrible scene in the pub after I barred someone who was dealing drugs. He'd come back at the end of the night and threatened to smash all the windows, told me I'd never be safe, that he'd find a way of getting to me. I'd thought I was used to the darker side of the pub, but I was feeling ground down by the fighting and the threats, and was discussing it with my parents in the bunga- low the next day when I started to shake. Pretty soon I was gasping for breath and my entire body was twitching – I had no control over it and I was terrified. My parents were worried but calm. They didn't like to think of me suffering, but looking after Matty had taught them how to cope with anything – this wasn't a big deal in comparison.

When it subsided, I went to sleep right there on the sofa in the bungalow for several hours. Mum made me an appointment at the doctor's and I was sent off for tests. It started to happen whenever I was upset or scared, and no one seemed to have a clue as to why. I told Sophie about it over the phone and she asked her dad what he thought. He said it sounded psychosomatic, that I might be having panic attacks and that the lack of oxygen was what was making me shake.

It was hard to accept that I was doing this to myself, but it sounded right. Mum suggested I go back and see Jane, and I did, every week, for a few months. The panic attacks became much less frequent, and I could usually head them off by practising the breathing techniques Jane taught me. She also thought my bowel problems were psychological. Her theory was that I felt guilty about the plan to move to London and abandon my family, so my mind and body were conspiring to keep me at home by making me too ill to leave.

Jane and I talked a lot about how difficult it was to deal with the knowledge that I wanted Matty to die. I knew it was the best thing for him, but I also wanted it for me. I wanted to be free from worry about him, and that made me feel unbearably guilty.

One night, as were picking our darts team, Carol said, 'Cora might not make it, and even if she does, she won't be in the mood for playing. She was burying her brother this morning.'

Cora was an elegant woman who wore cream silk blouses and drank halves of lager with lime. I imagined her standing on a mound of earth with a shovel in her hand and started laughing. All the ladies looked at me.

'I'm sorry,' I said. 'I was, you know, thinking of Cora with a shovel.'

They were still looking at me.

'You know, burying,' I said. 'I know it's not funny.' I was still laughing.

'Well,' said Carol, pursing her lips. She was very fond of me but I could see I had pushed her too far. 'You'd better not still be laughing if she comes in.'

I calmed down, we picked a team, and the evening continued. I can't remember the details – whether we beat the Black Lion 5-2 or got thrashed 6-1 by the Oddfellows – but there would have been seven games. We'd have cheered each other on by saying 'good arrows', and if the opposing player got a poor score, then we'd have said 'fill your boots' or 'dip your bread' to encourage our player to make the most of that moment of weakness. If anyone got stuck on double one – highly likely – they would have been told to 'think it's a field'. I'd have kept score, standing next to the board saying, 'OK, these go, game on,' and then calling out the totals and subtracting them on our electronic chalkie. We'd have done a raffle and handed round sandwiches. There might have been a corned-beef-and-pickle pie, a speciality of the player who had walked into the French windows at my graduation party. I would certainly have drunk a lot – pints of lager or Guinness or Moscow mules straight from the bottle. I would have smoked lots of cigarettes. I would probably have won my game because I usually did. So whilst there's much I can't remember, I do know that my laughter cloaked the extreme envy I felt for Cora. At that moment I had realized how desperate I was to bury my brother.

John was working as a recruitment consultant in emerging markets, and was living in London, in Rotherhithe, and either he would travel up at the weekends, or I would travel down to see him mid-week, setting off in the dead of night when I'd finished my shift behind the bar. One such night I got horribly lost coming into London and ended up in East Ham. After that, John bought me my first mobile phone. It had a contract for twelve months, which he said showed the level of his commitment to me. I knew he was thinking of proposing. He really wanted children, and I wasn't sure about it, but had said I could probably imagine having them when I was thirty.

One Friday, Dad and I picked John up from Leeds airport. He'd flown back from Kazakhstan via Frankfurt and Heathrow after a difficult trip during which he'd been threatened by a Kazak mafia person, so he'd started drinking on the plane and we decided to carry on.

Later that night he dragged me into the back kitchen and sat me down on a big, black speaker that had been left by one of the bands.

'Put down your cigarette,' he said, so I put it on the speaker. He put his down on his mobile phone.

He went down on one knee.

'Will you marry me?'

I wasn't sure I was wife material, but I loved him.

'Of course I will,' I replied.

The smell of burning plastic filled the air as my cigarette started to burn the speaker and his burnt into his phone, and then we went into the pub to tell everyone the news. No one was surprised.

'I've seen it for a long time,' said Carol. 'You two are made for each other.'

Mum and Dad were delighted. Dad wanted us to get

married straightaway, but I said I couldn't think of it while Matty was still alive.

1996 turned into 1997 and we decided that at last we must steel ourselves to apply to the court. We enlisted the help of our family solicitor Drummond Maxton, one half of Elmhirst and Maxton, a firm of Selby solicitors. He had overseen the purchase of our first house in Yorkshire in 1978, then the pub in 1989, and over the years had drawn up wills and offered advice. He was due to retire but said he wanted to help us, and would like to take this on as one of his last cases.

We told hardly anyone, only a tiny handful of Matty's friends, all of whom agreed it was the right thing to do. Everyone we did tell was always extremely supportive, but still we felt we had to be secretive. Dad's family were all Catholic so we assumed they would be against it on principle, and Mum was terrified that if people got to know, a band of religious protesters would turn up with placards and camp outside the door. We knew this had happened with Tony Bland, that a priest had tried to stop the withdrawal of nutrition going ahead.

We hated the idea of having to discuss it, explain it or justify it to all comers, who might only ask questions when pissed in the pub and not bother to listen to the answers. We didn't want it to be a topic of conversation, either at our bar or at any of the others in the area. After years of believing that where there was life, there was hope, we didn't want to have to try to explain how we'd changed our minds to people who hadn't travelled our hard road.

We had told Mr McEnroe that if the court agreed to our wishes, we intended to bring Matty home from Snaith Hall so neither he nor any of the staff would have to be involved. We asked him to tell no one.

Matty's was the fourteenth case of its kind to go before the court and the first ever to be taken by the family rather than the health authority. Because it was a court case there had to be a plaintiff and a defendant, so in legal terms it was Mum and Dad against Matty. It felt horrible. The Court of Protection appointed someone to act on Matty's behalf, and doctors came from 'both sides' to assess his condition. Mum had to write and swear an affidavit. Dad was still not very good at writing – he could manage shopping lists but with jumbled-up lower- and upper-case letters, he didn't have much idea about punctuation, and he wouldn't have been able to formulate his thoughts into written words. His affidavit simply said that he'd read his wife's and agreed.

I had to write my own and for the first and only time I felt a flicker of envy for my dad's lack of letters. I was supposed to be good at writing, but spent ages staring at the blank page. I tried to give myself a pep talk. It's only words, I thought. You only have to find some words – this isn't the hardest thing. Surely this is nothing compared with having to ring Mum from Pontefract, having to watch Matty fit, having to witness his bursting lung at Killingbeck, having to think of his vacant eyes staring out of his twisted body up at Snaith Hall. Surely this is nothing compared with the gradual erosion of hope. But it was hard. It felt wrong. Nothing in my life had prepared me for the task of having to write down that I wanted my brother to die.

I did it, though. By December 1997 everything was in place and the formal application to the court was made.

Affidavit of Margaret Anne Mintern

Sworn 18.12.1997

1

I am the mother of the defendant herein and make this affidavit in support of our application for an order/ declaration that our son Matthew Mintern the defendant herein may lawfully have discontinued all life-sustaining treatment and medical support measures withdrawn.

2

Matthew was born at teatime on Sunday 17 February 1974. He weighed in at 7 pounds twelve ounces after a problem-free and planned pregnancy. Kevin my husband and Matthew's father was present at the birth. He still rates Matthew's birth as the best experience of his life. When Catherine our daughter was born some thirteen months earlier he was unable to attend due to work commitments.

3

Matthew was a happy baby and from early on it was clear that he was very bright. He taught himself to tell the time at the age of 4 and was full of questions about the world around him. He was logical and intelligent.

4

At primary school he was popular with his peers, got on well with lessons and loved sport. He captained the school football team and won the *victor ludorum* in his final sports day. Secondary school was similarly happy. He had full attendance and became Senior Prefect, and in his final year he won the Headmaster's Prize for Outstanding Achievement, having gained 9 GCSEs, seven of those at Grade A.

5

In his leisure he played football for the same team from the age of 10 to the date of his accident. In his time with the team he won annual awards of Top Goal Scorer, Manager's Player of the year, and player of the year [voted by the team]. He also loved his pets and would spend hours patiently training his dog to do tricks.

6

Matthew was also very astute with money and purchased some British Gas shares out of his savings. When we bought our business in 1989 Matthew cashed in those shares and invested the £1000 to help with the purchase. He subsequently became a great help in the business, doing the cellar work before going to school, and helping out in the evenings and at weekends. He was popular with the customers, always being ready with a joke or a good story.

7

Matthew did not have a particular career in mind, but planned to study maths, physics and chemistry at Sixth Form College and thereafter to read science of some sort at university. His secondary school teachers suggested that he aim for Oxbridge.

8

During the summer of 1990 he obtained a seasonal job with Fairclough Engineering. They were impressed with him, and said they would fix him up with vacation work whilst he went through college and university.

9

Matthew was superb company, with a very quick sense of humour and a lively mind. He was hardworking and determined and very keen to do well in life. He loved sport both as a spectator, but mostly as a participant; we were enormously proud of him and loved him dearly.

10

Matthew was never to know how well he had done in his exams, because on 12 August 1990, some two weeks before the results came out, he was hit by a car. The first we knew of it was a phone call from Catherine, who had travelled with him in the ambulance. Catherine said to us 'they say it's serious, Mum; he's badly hurt'.

11

We waited together while he underwent emergency surgery, and then the surgeon came to talk to us. He explained to us what he had done and said that it was too early to give a prognosis. The next hours and days would be critical. If Matthew survived then the long-term prospects were not known. The surgeon had seen many people in Matthew's condition and, in his experience, many recovered but some didn't. At that time, the surgeon did warn us of the possibility of a 'vegetative' outcome. My immediate thoughts were 'Matthew will be one of the ones who recovers. He is fit, full of determination and loves life. He won't give up and neither will we.' Kevin, his father said 'He wouldn't want to be a cabbage' and he and Catherine cried inconsolably.

12

During the next three days Matthew was given drugs to sedate him to allow his brain to rest after the trauma and surgery. When the drugs were stopped we waited eagerly for Matthew to 'wake-up'. We were not unduly concerned when this did not happen immediately. We were told it could be weeks or even months. Many people told us stories of their loved ones returning from long periods of coma. After a few days Matthew came off the Intensive Care Ward, and shortly after he opened his eyes. We were ecstatic!

13

With the guidance of the experts we did all we could to aid
Matthew's recovery. On the physical side we learnt how to
keep his body flexible. We felt we were keeping it in shape
for when he would need it again. On the stimulation side
we tried everything, aiming to reach all five senses. We
spent all day with him, and were eventually able to take
him home for weekends.

14

Then his friends gathered and tried to coax him into
consciousness. People came to play guitars and sing to
him. We tried aromatherapy and reflexology, and even
allowed the dog to jump up on him.

15

Despite all the efforts of the professionals and ourselves,
Matthew failed to make any meaningful progress. A brain
scan was taken, which indicated hydrocephalus, and a
shunt was inserted to drain off the fluid. Shortly afterwards
the doctors decided to discontinue the epilepsy medication
he had been given routinely following a severe head injury.

16

About a month later Matthew had his first epileptic attack.
The small amount of progress he had made (occasionally
turning his head to a sound) was wiped out. I likened it to
a snail climbing up a wall and being knocked off. We went
back to square one.

17

This pattern continued. Small gains – the physiotherapist
noticed some 'holding tone' in his leg, he could swallow a
small amount of pureed food – and then an epileptic attack
would take it all away, leave his body tight and spastic,
and his awareness diminished. My diary entries for 1991
tell the sad story:

27 Feb. Took Matthew on corridors. Drinking really
good now. Ribena quite a favourite. Kev got a full litre in
during the day. Physio good. Stood on mat, left foot much
better – and got right arm onto table. Alan (senior
physiotherapist) able to let go at both sides of pelvis – only
possible on left before. Another fit at 19.45 – just when we
seemed to be getting somewhere.

6 March. Matthew has not recovered from the fit last
week and has definitely gone backwards. No longer able
to swallow, so completely fed by tube again. Ability to
'follow' also lost – eyes quite vacant. It's like going back
3–4 months.

18

One morning we arrived as usual at the hospital to find the
curtains drawn round Matthew's bed and the staff looking
sombre. The doctor explained that Matthew had suffered
a bad fit – status epilepticus – and was very poorly. He
asked what we wanted him to do. I realized with horror
that he was asking whether he should treat Matthew or let
him die. Our response was unequivocal: 'Treat him. He is
our loved son. He may yet get better.' Some time after this

incident we asked to have him home permanently. He
seemed more settled on the weekends when he was at
home. The staff taught us all we needed to know to care
for him and he came home in May. My diary entry that day
reads 'A busy month arranging to bring Matthew home.
Feel very sad. Have had bereavement without a death.
No real change in Matthew's condition – tube fed entirely
– chest much better – eyes not focusing or following, but
no longer pulled to right. Right arm severely flexes – may
have lost it altogether at elbow and wrist-contractures.
Love him with all my heart.' We built a ground-floor
extension and had everything science and technology
had to offer: special chairs, lifting equipment,
physiotherapy and stimulation equipment, the services
of a physiotherapist, occupational therapist and speech
therapist. We visited the Royal Hospital and Home at
Putney, who specialize in brain injury cases. The senior
doctor there said there was nothing more he could
suggest; Matthew's regime could not be improved.
Did we have space to take some of his patients?

19

Despite all our efforts Matthew did not improve. A brain
scan, undertaken to explore the epilepsy, had shown
that the brain tissue had shrunk since the last scan. The
conclusion was that we could expect no improvement.
It occurred to me that all we were doing was not only
pointless but potentially harmful. The more we did with
Matthew the more likely he was to have a fit. The fits were

terrible. He would start with a terrified scream – the only time we ever heard him make any significant sound – then move into a grand mal. After the fit he would have a long period of shaking, overheating, and extreme spasticity, with a pulse rate so fast it could not be counted. We consulted another epilepsy specialist, who tried new medications, but the fits persisted. In discussion with the medical team we decided to change our emphasis to 'palliative care' rather than 'rehabilitation', with the object of our care being to keep Matthew without pain or distress.

20

During the spring of 1995 I reached a very low ebb. I had been jollying everyone along for so long but realized there was no point to it all. On Matthew's 21st birthday people brought in cards and presents (What do you give to someone in Matthew's state? How do you 'celebrate' his 21st?) I sat with Matthew and read his cards to him, and opened his presents, knowing that he understood nothing, but keeping up the show for everyone else's benefit. The school choir came to sing for him, and I had to pretend that he enjoyed it. I felt that I was living a lie. In addition, I was deeply tired. I had given everything to get Matthew back, and it was not to be. I was left with a deep emotional tiredness that no amount of sleep would cure. I was broken. I had no time to dream of Matthew before the injury and each time I awoke it was to face anew the horror of his situation.

21

Awaking one morning after dreaming of Matthew, I realized that if he could see what we were putting ourselves through for the sake of his poor twisted body, he would say that we were crazy. It was then that I first considered transferring him to a nursing home. This was the most difficult decision of all. It represented failure, and I felt ashamed. I had vowed that Matthew would always be cared for at home, and, once I realized he was not going to recover, I wanted him to die at home, surrounded by those who loved him. His care was breaking me, and it was all for nothing. He did not know who he was, where he was, or who we were. Why were we doing it?

22

I visited several nursing homes in the area, and decided the most suitable was in our own village. They knew of Matthew and all we had tried. They had no problem with Matthew having his own private nurse to come in just for him. The home had no vacancies at the time, but when one became available in August we moved him in. Relinquishing the daily care to the nursing home gave me the opportunity to begin to mourn Matthew. His physical removal from our home enabled me to remember the son we had lost; the tall 16-year-old, confident, fit and intelligent. It was then I saw how wrong the current situation was. Matthew would never want to be kept alive in this pitiable and hopeless condition. He had prided himself on his intellect and physical prowess. Now he lay, eyes vacant, food pumped into one end and coaxed out with suppositories at the other, unable to make any communication or know any joy. A living corpse. It was unhealthy and unnatural.

23

After many hours of discussion, Kevin, Catherine and I decided that we should seek permission to discontinue nutrition and hydration. We approached our GP in December 1996 and received his support and approval. We spoke to close family members and Matthew's closest friends, and everyone thought it was for the best. We approached the owner of the nursing home to put him in the picture, and he informed us that Matthew was quite poorly with a chest infection, and suggested that we wait for a while. Matthew recovered from the chest problem without the intervention of antibiotics, so in the spring of 1997 we approached our family solicitor, Mr Maxton. We asked Mr Myles Gibson to examine Matthew as he was aware of his condition, and we knew and trusted him. For my part I wanted an expert opinion from someone who knew how much we loved Matthew. Mr Myles Gibson was very thorough and very kind, and when his report confirmed Matthew was in a permanent vegetative state we felt ready to move on. On the advice of our barrister we asked Professor Jennett to examine Matthew. He agreed that Matthew was in a permanent vegetative state. Professor Jennett was also very kind, and I felt able to ask him many questions. I wanted to know whether today, 7 years on, doctors could be any more precise on the initial prognosis. Could someone say, on the day of the injury, 'There is no hope for your son.' The Professor said that doctors would still not be able to know in the early days how each case would turn out. I also asked him what would actually happen to Matthew if we withdrew nutrition and hydration. He said that in most cases it is a very peaceful process, with full coma occurring after a few days, and death within another week or so. I told him that I had always wanted Matthew to die at home, and he said that other relatives have felt this and have taken the patient home. He said he was very willing to give our GPs any advice they may need. All in all Professor Jennett's visit took a lot of the uncertainty and fear from me and I felt happy that Matthew after all would be able to die at home.

24

I have known for some time that there is nothing I can do for Matthew to enrich his life in any way. He needs to die. We had hoped it would happen with an infection and without the need to approach the court. But the sad irony is that his poor body, unable to do anything else, seems capable of fighting infection. So we are asking the court's permission to cease nutrition and hydration so that Matthew can be released from his hopeless state. It is our last act of love for him.

25

If the court agrees we would like to nurse Matthew ourselves with the assistance of the lady who has been his private nurse in the nursing home. Sue knew Matthew before the injury and has been involved in his care since 1992. She has always treated him with the utmost respect and dignity. She is a perfect nurse. We cared for Matthew at home for over 4 years, and still have all the specialist equipment. We have the support of our GPs who themselves have the offer of advice from Professor Jennett. We feel it is fitting for Matthew and best for us if he is able to die at home.

RE M (A MINOR)

The court hearing was scheduled for 16 June 1998 at the Royal Courts of Justice on the Strand. By this time my health had improved a bit and I was living in London with John in a flat on Little Russell Street, just across the road from the British Museum. I wasn't working – I'd done some temping and admin jobs but hated them all. I couldn't think of anything I wanted to do and was terrified of going to interviews. My parents were giving me an allowance and had suggested that I shouldn't worry about my own future until after Matty's death.

Mum and Dad travelled down on the train the day before and stayed in the President Hotel in Russell Square. That night we all went to the theatre to see *Show Boat*. I cried through 'Can't help lovin' dat man of mine', and when I looked over at them I saw that they were too.

John took the day off work to come to the court with us. We were all suited and booted, as they'd say in the pub, but only John looked natural. The rest of us looked a bit 'dressed-up'. We were nervous, rather overawed, and relieved to see Mr Maxton waiting for us on the steps. He explained that we would meet up with the rest of the legal team inside. As we prepared to go in, Linford Christie arrived for his libel hearing, the one where a bemused Justice Popplewell announced himself unfamiliar with the term 'lunchbox', and bounded up the steps ahead of us.

'Well, if we're in the same court he'll get there first,' said Dad.

We were ushered up a magnificent staircase to an upstairs room. Mum was the plaintiff and waited to be called to give evidence. She was wearing a brown tweed suit that she had bought in Scotland before travelling down to Cornwall for my granddad's funeral in 1982.

Once inside the court everyone was extremely kind to us. The various judicial people went out of their way to comment on the level of care Matty had received, that nothing more could possibly have been done. There was no doubt that he was in a Permanent Vegetative State, and that his condition was never going to improve.

The judge was asked whether he would like Mum called as a witness.

'I don't think we need put Mrs Mintern through that,' he said. 'She has been through enough.'

The judge read his ruling. He agreed that Matty should die. I felt strangely calm as the rather beautifully phrased words washed over me, relieved that here were people who had applied intelligence and empathy to our situation and understood that this was a horrible but necessary duty that we had to carry out to liberate Matty from the prison of his body.

And that was it. We thanked everyone and left the court. We went to the pub across the road, the Royal George, and had a gin and tonic each, and then Mum and Dad set off back to Yorkshire. John and I went out and got drunk.

The court had decided that it was the right thing to do. The only thing left was the doing of it.

All England Official Transcripts (1997–2008)

Re M (a minor)
(Transcript: Harry Counsell)

FAMILY DIVISION

SIR STEPHEN BROWN (P)

16 JUNE 1998
H Lloyd for the First and Second Plaintiffs;
M Hinchliffe for the Official Solicitor
Elmhurst & Maxton

SIR STEPHEN BROWN (P):

This is a distressing case which has given rise to an application by the parents of a young man who is now 24, but who suffered a serious road accident injury as long ago as 1990. He is in what the experienced medical witnesses have described as a "permanent vegetative state".

Professor Jennett, who has perhaps more experience than anybody else – except perhaps Dr Andrews – of this condition, has no doubt that he is in a permanent vegetative state, and has been in that condition now for several years with no hope of recovery.

The application made is that the court should grant a declaration that plaintiffs and the responsible medical practitioners having the care of this young man may lawfully discontinue all life-sustaining treatment and medical support measures, including nutrition and hydration by artificial means, designed to keep "M" alive in his existing permanent vegetative state, and may lawfully furnish such treatment and nursing care under medical supervision as may be appropriate to ensure that "M" suffers the least distress and retains the greatest dignity until such time as his life comes to an end.

I have observed that it is a distressing case, particularly moving, because this young man in his young life had achieved so much and showed great promise for the future. I have before me a lengthy affidavit sworn by his mother who has given him remarkable care over the past seven years. It is a very moving account of how the family had to face the appalling tragedy which confronted them, and how they had to live with the day-to-day knowledge which grew upon them, that there would be no hope of recovery.

They had at the beginning optimism and hope and one can well understand it, but the initial grave condition was exacerbated quite shortly afterwards by the onset of epilepsy. By 1992 this young man was experiencing epileptic fits fortnightly.

The medical attention has been superb and intensive. He was initially in intensive care in hospital. There came a time in April, 1991 when he was taken home and nursed there by his mother, and eight or nine devoted care attendants, all of course under the supervision not only of the General Practitioner, whose affidavit evidence I have before me, but also of the Consultant Neurosurgeon who saw him on frequent occasions and who has reported on no less than six occasions and I have his affidavit evidence before me.

There is no doubt in my mind having heard and read all the evidence that for several years now this young man has been wholly unaware of anything that goes on about him. It is one of the features of this condition that there are reflex responses which can give to those unaccustomed with dealing with these matters, a false idea of the patient's actual condition.

In this case there was, of course, another feature, that is to say, because this young man had suffered injuries as a pedestrian by being knocked down by a motor vehicle there was claim for damages, and that had to be investigated by those pursuing the claim. The Court of Protection has been involved and, of course, the insurance company representing the driver of the motor vehicle. They had to make their inquiries and one step that they took was to instruct a Neurologist who examined this patient and I have before me Reports of 1992 and 1993 in which that Doctor seemed to indicate that there was some degree of awareness. But as has been pointed out by Dr Howe, to whom I shall refer in due course, in these reports it rather seems as though that Doctor was describing rather more what he had been told than what he actually observed himself.

Of course those matters have put the Official Solicitor, and indeed the plaintiffs' doctors on inquiry, and hence, of course, the instruction of Professor Jennett as a totally independent and experienced expert in this field, and also of Dr Howe, a Consultant Neurologist of great experience in this field. He was, in fact, the Consultant Neurologist who had the initial responsibility for the care of Mr Bland, whose case was the first to come before the courts in this area.

I have heard the oral evidence of Professor Jennett, and of Dr Howe. Both these witnesses are in no doubt at all that this is a classic case of the persistent vegetative state. There is no awareness; there is an indication of some nystagmus which Professor Jennett describes as a confusing matter, and has been described by Dr Howe as being recognized now as something that can be generated by the brain stem. In recent research which he has conducted himself by investigating with others in this condition, he has made it plain that that is not a matter which can indicate real living awareness.

The parents and sister of "M" have no doubt whatsoever of their daily observations, and they of all people are most in touch with him, that this is not a "living person" – I put that in inverted commas – but merely the body shell of a spirit who no longer exists in this world. It is a very sad case indeed.

Every case which gives rise to the permanent vegetative state is distressing, but I believe this to be particularly distressing to these caring parents who have in their minds only the best interests of their son. They have not undertaken these proceedings lightly. Indeed, it is quite plain from the lengthy affidavit of the mother that there has been a very great deal of heart searching in the past, but they have come to the conclusion that it is in the best interests of their son that his physical existence should now be allowed to come to an end in a dignified manner.

I have heard Mr Hinchliffe, who appears for the Official Solicitor, who has conducted the fullest inquiries on behalf of this patient who cannot, of course, instruct anybody himself. This has been investigated with the very greatest care and I am quite satisfied that it is a case of permanent vegetative state, that it has existed now for several years, and that there is no possibility of any recovery or improvement. In these circumstances it is in the best interests of "M" that these declarations should be granted, and I propose to grant them.

I would like to express my appreciation of the tremendous care which has been given to "M" by his mother, father and sister, and to express, what I am sure all those in court will wish to be associated with, the very greatest admiration for their courage and the care which they have given to him. I believe that the time has come when the reality of the position must be recognized, and accordingly I make the declarations.

Application granted.

DEATH COMES AS THE END

On Tuesday 23 June 1998, Matty made his last homecoming. We told no one about the withdrawal because we were still worried that religious protesters would try to stop it. We just said that Matty was very poorly and had come home to die.

We'd discussed how we could cope with it in a way that reminded me of coming home in the car the morning after the accident. Mum and Dad made a plan that she would look after Matty, and Dad would look after her. I would stay in London for a few days and then travel up to Yorkshire on Friday with John after he finished work. That would be day four of withdrawal and by then Matty should be in full coma. I envisaged sitting by his bed, holding his hand, being with him as he slipped away. I'd talk him through his last hours with childhood stories, the way I used to. I hoped that once in deep coma, I'd be able to see the lost Matty in his sleeping face. I wanted to try to forget the eight years that had passed since that night in the road, to remember him as he was and to be able to mourn him.

I phoned my parents two or three times a day and they talked me through everything they were doing. They worked out what equipment they needed to bring back from the nursing home: the electrically operated bed, the ripple mattress, the hoist, convenes, urine bags, medications. They didn't need the feeding paraphernalia as the withdrawal was to start straightaway. Mum went up to the nursing home and helped Sue to bathe Matty, whilst Dad transferred the bed and mattress to the bungalow, then came back for Matty. His bed was put back at the side of Mum's and Dad's, and they tried to make the room look as little like a hospital as possible: freesias on the windowsill, World Cup commentary on the radio. Mum had set herself up with a table and a jigsaw to keep her company through the coming hours.

Dr Howe had told them what to expect. He said there would be an increase in reflex motor activity because of an increase in adrenaline stimulating the brain stem's motor reflexes. After two or three days, Matty's eyes would close and a coma state would come in. The whole process would take seven to ten days, and if the patient had been well looked-after up to the time of treatment withdrawal, it would be on the longer side.

He said that Matty's death would probably occur because of kidney failure (increase in potassium) and/or a chest infection (decrease in oxygen in the blood). Both act to stop the heart. We would know we were near the end when his breathing rate increased. The GP would call every few days, and Dr Howe said we could ring him any time. The GP said to use diazepam as a sedative as often as necessary, and not to let Matty be uncomfortable at all. It was important that no fluids were administered. There was a gel called glandosane to put on his lips to stop them cracking.

When I rang on Thursday I could hear the stress in Mum's voice, though she was trying to sound upbeat.

'He's still awake and making quite a lot of noise, but he should go into coma soon.'

She had used up all the diazepam and had been upset when the chemist hadn't had any earlier in the day. She had rung for a prescription, rung the chemist to check they had it, collected the prescription from the surgery, but when she called at the chemist found they had none in stock.

'Sorry to be so self-pitying,' she said to me, 'but it doesn't seem a lot to ask when we are doing so much ourselves.'

When John and I arrived at the pub late on Friday night, I went into the bungalow and John went straight upstairs. I'd met John after Matty had moved to Snaith Hall so John had never seen him, and I didn't want him to see him now. It was in my mind to protect them both. Matty didn't need to be observed by yet more people, and I didn't want John to be faced with the devastating sight of what a blow to the head could do to a human being. I explained this to John and he agreed to leave me to it.

Mum and Dad looked tired and drawn and Matty was asleep. This was the first time I'd seen him since just after he'd gone to the nursing home almost three years ago. Three years in which I'd tried to get on with life and Matty had stayed still. I felt more strongly than ever that no human being should be made to linger on in a deteriorating body when the brain has gone. Mum said she hoped that this sleep might be the start of the coma that would lead to his death.

The next morning I could hear Matty as I went into the bungalow. He was making a low groaning sound, a constant 'Uh-uh, uh-uh.' When Dr Howe rang he was surprised that he was not yet in coma five days in. He said it could be that Matty was a bit overweight and fat cells hold a lot of water, but he said he still expected the whole process to be over within ten days.

John went back to London after the weekend and I stayed for another five days. Nothing changed. No coma, no peaceful ending. Mum looked after Matty while Dad and I took Murphy down to the riverbank and went to the pub together. We played lots of games of darts. At one point Dad got three 180s on the bounce, a pretty amazing achievement, though his grim expression didn't alter.

I thought of all the years growing up when we'd had a dartboard in the house at Almond Tree Avenue and Dad used to take me and Matty on all the time. He wouldn't let us win but would always give us a good start so we had a fighting chance. He'd also take us up to the pub and teach us to play pool. I always had the edge over Matty at darts; he was better than me at pool. When I was seventeen I became the youngest ever winner of the Snaith and District Ladies' Darts Championship. We all went to the club at Drax Power Station for the finals. I threw a 180, for which I'd get an extra trophy, and Dad was so proud when I finished – on double sixteen, my favourite – that he bounded onto the stage and picked me up in his arms. I couldn't connect anything about that family then with what we'd become over the eight years since Matty's accident.

Still, the darts, while not giving us pleasure, gave us something to do. Being honest by nature, it was difficult for us to be with people, given that we weren't able to tell them the full story. I kept wondering what people would say if they knew, if I just blurted it out.

'How's your kid?'

'We're starving him to death right now. His kidneys might be ceasing to function this very second.'

I tried to sit and talk to Matty but found it very hard and couldn't bear to look into his eyes. All those years I'd stared into them looking for his soul, and now I hoped he'd never had any awareness of his awful situation, that his soul hadn't been trapped there, suffering.

Looking down at his arms, I realized that the scars from the accident had completely healed. I remembered the priest who told us that the fact that Matty's hair grew meant he'd get better. I stared at Matty's body, his twisted arm and foot. This healing of scars was the one positive thing that had happened to him physically.

On the tenth day Dad found me crying in the bungalow and suggested I go back to John.

'You're breaking your heart here. There's nothing you can do. Don't tear yourself apart.'

One of our customers drove me to Doncaster station and I took the train back to London. I was in agonies of sobbing. I curled up in a little ball and cried all the way. A couple of people asked if they could help, but I just shook my head.

'I'm sorry,' I choked out. 'I'm sorry. Please just leave me alone.'

The news came on Sunday, thirteen days after we had started the withdrawal. I was sitting on the sofa when my dad rang. I can't remember what I did in the three days between getting back to London and taking the call. It feels like I just sat on the sofa and stared at the phone.

'It's over, Ca. He's gone. Poor old chap.'

He asked me if I was all right, and I could hear the worry in his voice. I remembered seeing the worry on Matty's face that day I fell off his motorbike and knowing it was a sign of love. I thought of when I'd had to ring Mum from Pontefract on the night of the accident. I thought what a terrible thing to have to do as a father, to ring your daughter to say that your son, her brother, is dead, and to worry how she will cope with it.

'I'll be OK, Dad,' I said. 'I'll be OK.'

THE LONG COFFIN

I woke up crying on the day of Matty's funeral. I cried my way through putting on my white blouse, my black trousers, my little black ballet pumps, cried as we assembled in the street outside our pub in the hot sun. Mum and Dad. John and Sophie, Frank, Liz and Sue. I knew I was surrounded by love as we walked up the street to the church, following the big, black, shiny hearse and followed in turn by our friends and customers.

At the church, there was a problem as the undertakers tried to manoeuvre the long coffin out of the car and onto the shoulders of Matty's friends. There was a little stumble, and I thought they were going to drop him. And it was funny. I felt like I'd seen it before, in *Only Fools and Horses* or *Last of the Summer Wine*. For just a moment I wanted to laugh rather than cry.

Of course the coffin was long because Matty was long. I thought of how his height – all six feet and four inches of him – had been such a source of pride to us all when he was upright and then so problematic after the accident. He had had to have a special extension built on the end of his hospital bed. The shorter physiotherapists and nurses had struggled. 'Isn't he long?' people would say as they looked down at him in a bed, on a mat, in a shower trolley. Not tall, any more, but long. And here again his length was causing problems.

They didn't drop him, Matty's friends, the boys who had grown up with him, played football with him, drunk vodka with him. The boys who had visited him in hospital and then at home until it gradually became clear to everyone that he had no idea they were there. They delivered him safely into the church, we filed our way to the front, and the vicar said some kind things about Matty, about us, and about the love that he saw in our family.

He told a story about Matty's competitive streak, about how in biology class at school he snapped his friend Lizzie's broad bean because it was growing faster than his. There was a ripple of laughter and a feeling of relief. He was doing a good job, the vicar, because who knows what to say in this situation? How do you find something to say about someone who hasn't demonstrated any of their considerable personality for the last eight years?

As the sun shone through the stained-glass windows making beautiful patterns on the floor and dust motes drifted in the air, the vicar talked about Matty dying with his parents and his sister by his side. But this wasn't true. It should have been, but I couldn't hack the final days and it was Sue who had been with my parents when Matty died. The vicar's mistake was making me feel even more of a useless fraud than I already did. I wasn't there, I kept thinking as the tears ran down my cheeks, I wasn't there.

There were hymns. 'Abide with Me' and 'Dear Lord and

Father of Mankind', which was Mum's favourite – she'd chosen it for both her wedding and her father's funeral. My uncle did a reading, 1 Corinthians 13, about how the greatest thing is love.

We left the church and got into the car that would take us to the crematorium.

Dad said, 'Thank God that's over. Now we can get on with planning your wedding.'

I stared out of the window.

I can't remember much of what happened at the crematorium. I've been to other funerals since and they've jumbled up in my mind. I can't remember if the coffin trundled off on a conveyor belt – does that ever actually happen? – or if the curtains were simply drawn around it. I can see faded blue velvet curtains with a brocade trim in my mind, but I can't swear that it was Matty's coffin they shrouded. I know I stared at the coffin for a good long time as we listened to Mozart and I wondered about who would be in charge of the next stage. How would the coffin get into an oven, how would that long, tall, body be reduced to a pile of ash? I wondered if Matty's pile of ash would be bigger than the pile of ash you'd get from a shorter person. I started to feel sick. At least we were burning him, I thought. At one time I'd liked the idea of burying him in the churchyard, but I'd have been even less able to cope with the idea of him rotting away under the ground.

And then it was over. We walked out into sunshine. I could see some suited men, functionaries of some type, smoking behind the bushes. Sue gave me a cuddle, her kind face full of love. I sobbed into her shoulder. I still felt bad about the vicar's mistake, but I didn't know how to say it to her. She'd been lavishing care on me as well as Matty for years and I wanted to say thank you, but I couldn't find the words.

Then it was back into the black cars which would return us to the pub. There were people to be entertained, in that strange way that a funeral makes hosts of the next of kin. We'd been a long time waiting for this wake – there was drink to be drunk and stories to be told.

By this time, I was a long way from laughter.

'LIVING DEATH' TORMENT OF FAMILY

Gifted schoolboy Matthew Mintern finally died on Sunday, aged 24, eight years after an accident left him in a persistent vegetative state.

When Matthew Mintern's GCSE results came through in 1990 he was confirmed as one of the brightest boys in his school.

But the 6ft 4in talented sportsman never recovered from a road accident to discover he had achieved eight A grades and two Bs.

Eight years ago, as he made his way home after a night out, Matthew suffered horrific head injuries when he was hit by a motorist, later prosecuted for careless driving.

Back then his parents Margaret, now 44, and Kevin, 48, and sister Cathy believed and hoped that one day he would recover. What followed was an eight-year nightmare in which the family tried every conceivable treatment and device to rouse Matthew.

'Over the years we tried everything – reflexology, physiotherapy, music, using computers to track Matty's eye movement,' explained Cathy, to whom he was very close.

Medical opinion now suggests he was in a persistent vegetative state (PVS) soon after the accident, the same condition as suffered by Hillsborough stadium disaster victim Tony Bland.

It means that part of the brain which controls talking and thinking has been irrevocably damaged. But Cathy says that in 1990 there was talk about the condition PVS, although she suspects doctors realized there was no chance of Matthew 'waking up.'

'I think people knew a long time before we did it was a no-go situation.'

The family's hopes were raised soon after surgery when his eyes opened. His head occasionally moved and small amounts of food could be swallowed.

After nine months in hospital he was brought home to live above the pub, the Bell and Crown at Snaith, East Yorkshire, which his parents still run. It required 24-hour dedication as he had to be fed, washed and clothed several times a day.

'It was terribly hard,' recalls Miss Minter, at 25 a year older than her brother.

'We were all so confident that he would recover. I suppose blindly and stupidly we thought that enough love and enough effort would make him well. Everyone put so much work into trying to make him better.'

[. . .]

Last month the family brought Matthew home to die. Thirteen days after all hydration, nutrition and medication was withdrawn he died with mother, father and a nurse present.

A funeral service at Snaith Priory Church yesterday was followed by cremation at Pontefract crematorium.

Yorkshire Post, 10 July 1998

The day after the funeral, Carol phoned through to the bungalow. A girl from the local paper was at the bar and wanted to talk to us about Matty.

Dad asked me if I could speak to her.

'What shall I tell her?'

'Just tell her the truth. Everything.'

So I sat with the girl in the back room of the pub and watched as she converted my attempts to explain the gradual erosion of hope into squiggles of shorthand in her notebook. After the story came out, lots of other papers rang up and I talked to them all. It was a relief to have our secret out in the world and our customers were lovely to us, though a few people were cross that we hadn't told them about it ourselves.

'I don't think I should have had to read about it in the paper,' said one of Matty's friends who hadn't visited him for years. I shrugged. I didn't know what to tell her. I felt a bit sorry for her but she hadn't been at the top of our extremely long list of things to worry about, that was all.

Everyone kept saying how strong I was, what a support to my parents, but I didn't feel that way at all. There was a surface me who could smile and talk to people, but underneath I was only a few seconds away from splintering into tiny pieces and floating away on the air. I didn't know what was going to happen next. I didn't know how I was going to live in the world. I kept having nightmares that Matty was alive and banging on the lid of his coffin underground, that he was rotting away, that he was chasing me and wanted me to get into the grave with him.

I had expected a sense of relief and kept telling the reporters that it was a relief that Matty had finally died, but I didn't feel it. I thought that once Matty was dead the pain of worrying about his suffering would ease. I thought I had done all my grieving – I seemed to have been crying constantly for the last eight years so I was unprepared for the further avalanche of grief and guilt.

And I was surprised. I'd experienced plenty of pain over the years, but none of it – after the night of the accident – had been surprising. Now I was full of a swirling and incomprehensible anguish I'd never anticipated. I didn't know what to do with myself.

I didn't tell anyone about this. I tried to show a happy face to the world, including my parents, who were both exhausted and ill. The only people who knew the real story were John and Sophie. They were used to being my confidants and looking after me.

'It takes a year to get over a death,' one of our customers said, and I thought of all those novels I'd read where people wore black gloves for a period of mourning. A year, I thought. There have already been eight unspeakably shitty years. I just have to get through one more, and then I won't feel like this.

'Now we can get on with planning your wedding,' Dad had said on the way to the crematorium. He loved John and he wanted me to be happy. I'd felt it was impossible to get married when Matty was alive, but now I drifted towards it. It was something to do.

I organized it for the following September, when I thought I'd be healed. We booked Carlton Towers, where I'd daydreamed in the library, where Matty and Didge had taught themselves to drive off-road in their little Fiat. We invited 170 guests and I tried to be enthusiastic about choosing what sort of flowers would decorate the church, what we would eat. I planned several courses with a *trou normand* and a *croquembouche*. I didn't want to wear a white dress as I thought I'd look like an idiot, so I left it until the last minute and then bought a grey silk trouser suit from Monsoon. A friend from the pub painted my nails silver and put some make-up on me, and I wore the same black ballet pumps I'd worn at Matty's funeral. I cried my way up the aisle of the church, and the same vicar who had buried Matty married John and me. We got a double-decker bus to the Towers and everyone from my side got very drunk.

The next day we threw an enormous party in the pub, a feast with oysters, lobsters and shell-on prawns.

'They're all right, these prawns,' said one of our customers to Dad. 'Bit crunchy, though.' He didn't know you were supposed to peel them.

Back in London, I waited to feel fixed. A year had passed. I was married. I was due my happy ending.

Instead, I cried every day for three or four months. I had no idea what was wrong with me.

John was travelling more with work and sometimes I went with him. I'd learned in the pub how to strike up a conversation with anyone, and I could do the same with all John's colleagues and clients. I liked the bustle of Hong Kong and the novelistic feel of the ex-pat community, but I was in a continual state of panic in South America due to the awful driving and the large insects. One especially reckless taxi driver had a bunch of religious medallions hanging from his rear-view mirror. I said a Hail Mary in my head and did my breathing exercises. I remembered being in the chapel and noted my continuing habit of turning to religion in times of extremis. We got safely to our destination and I felt relieved that my parents wouldn't get a phone call to tell them I'd died on the road in a faraway land.

Back in London, John and I drank a lot in the pub at the end of Little Russell Street, the Plough, and one day the landlord asked if I would help out with a couple of shifts as he'd been let down. I started working from 12 till 5 during the week, and found it was good to be back behind a bar again. My favourite customers were a group of builders, and when I finished my shift I'd sit on the other side of the bar with them and drink pints of Guinness. They taught me how to do the cryptic crossword in the *Telegraph*. John wasn't massively impressed with all this, especially as I was always several sheets to the wind when he came home from work, and he began to lose patience with my insatiable appetite for booze and new people. He was growing up, moving on, taking himself and his career seriously while I was still behaving like a student. I was often useful, though. One night John rang me from Quo Vadis, where he was entertaining a diverse group of foreign work contacts to dinner, to say, 'They won't talk to each other. Can you come down and liven it all up a bit.' So I did.

I was doing some writing, and one of my customers in the Plough sent a few chapters to a publisher who liked what I'd done and wanted to see more. I got the call from the publisher on the same day that John was asked to set up an office in New York for the recruitment company he worked for. We went out for dinner to discuss it. Why not? we thought. I phoned my parents, who were very pleased.

Here, I thought, was our happy ending. We arrived in New York just in time for the fourth of July celebrations in 2000, and found an apartment in Chelsea with a 24-hour bookstore at the end of the street. John worked long hours and I'd write during the day and then join him and his colleagues or clients in the evening for drinks and dinner. I enjoyed talking to them about work. Recruitment is about people, after all, and there were plenty of good stories about the peculiar habits of sought-after candidates. One man, whose wife didn't want him to take up a job offer in another country, decided to plump for the job rather than the wife.

I loved the open nature of New Yorkers and found it easy to make friends. They liked bookish English girls. I'd never thought of myself as looking Irish, but people would regularly ask me if I was and were pleased with the answer. When friends came over from England, we would take them for cocktails at Windows on the World at the top of the World Trade Center, and then out for steak or lobster.

You can get anything you want in New York, but you have to be specific. Instead of asking for a Martini, you need to ask for a vodka Martini, very dry, straight up with a twist. I smoked white-tipped Lucky Strike Lights and loved that you could call up the grocery store and get them to deliver booze and fags. We ate a lot of takeout Chinese and delighted in the cute little boxes and fortune cookies that made us feel like we were in an episode of *Friends*. I adopted the language: I liked that I lived in an apartment, rode the elevator, got the check, drank mimosas and did brunch.

I didn't have a work visa, which made me feel less of a failure for not having a job. And the writing was going well. I was quite happy, though it felt a bit like a dream. One day, as I was walking down Fifth Avenue, snow started to fall, and I suddenly thought, *I'm not real. I'm in a film about an English girl walking down Fifth Avenue in the snow. I'm not real.*

After a year, John's company asked if he would relocate to Chicago and move into the telecoms side of the business, leaving recruiting behind. There was a gap of a few weeks, so we came back to London where John worked out of his old office and I went out a lot with Sophie, who was living in London and working as a journalist.

We were both at home on 11 September 2001, because John was off sick with tonsillitis, when a friend called and told us to turn on the TV. We watched the Twin Towers fall again and again. Everyone phoned us, worrying we might still be there. For most of that day and the weeks that followed I really thought I was dreaming or having an episode. The world suddenly seemed too full of pain.

It was a relief to be on the move again, and in October that year we moved into the top floor of a white wooden house in the western suburbs of Chicago. We had a picket fence and a mailbox at the foot of the lawn. There was none of the joy of being in New York. America as a nation was grieving and suspicious and it was difficult to be there as a foreigner.

It was the law in the state of Illinois that you had to show ID when buying alcohol. 'This ID is from out of state,' people would say, staring at us resentfully in supermarkets, liquor stores and bars. We'd always get the booze in the end but it often felt like they'd rather be phoning the police to have us arrested for being foreign.

I tried to get on with my novel, but everything seemed irrelevant. My main character had worked in the South Tower, so either she was dead, or she had more to worry about than the fictional problems I'd been subjecting her to. I'd made the mistake of introducing a character based on Matty. He wasn't essential to the plot, but I kept thinking of ways to make the book more about him and torturing myself by trying to imagine what he would have been like as he grew older.

I toyed with the idea of a novel about the death of a relationship, but couldn't start it. Deep down I feared that the novel writing was a pretence, that I wasn't capable of it; I just didn't want to be forced to do something else. I spent the mornings sleeping off my daily hangover and then woke up and read detective novels or sat at the kitchen table in my pyjamas, playing countless games of Minesweeper on my laptop, watching the double-decker trains go by and wondering if I'd like to be on one. Yes, I thought, because I'd like to be doing something different, and no, because I was frightened of almost everything. I felt like my own dull, rather saccharine storyline could veer off into thriller territory at any moment. If I were to get on one of those trains, I'd end up buried under the floorboards of someone called Jed or Buck.

John was bewildered by my failure to enjoy America, my lack of enthusiasm for his suggestions that we go skiing in Aspen, or sailing on Lake Michigan, hire a Cadillac and drive to New Orleans for Mardi Gras. He didn't say so directly, but I knew he thought that I had grieved enough. I agreed with him entirely that that should be true, but wanting something didn't make it so, and no amount of counting my blessings – and I did try. I lay in bed at night listening to his breathing and counting blessings like fat sheep – made me feel anything other than ungrateful.

Most nights we went out to dinner in one of the restaurants in our little town. We'd have two cocktails each and share a bottle of wine as John talked about work. There were no interesting stories in telecoms so he'd try to explain about routers and trans-Atlantic cables. I can't remember what dense wave divisional multiplexing is, but I know he told me. Then we'd go home and he'd sit on the sofa and fight terrorists on his PlayStation while I opened another bottle of wine and got back to not writing my novel.

Winter set in. It was so cold that it hurt to breathe and I was frightened of being in a car on the snowy roads. In the spring all the supermarkets introduced displays with snake and rodent traps and I developed a distrust of our garden and of what might be loitering in the longer grass.

When I went home for a holiday, I lied to all our customers and friends. I was fine, John was fine, Chicago was great, the book was coming along nicely. There was one night, when I was drunk, that I thought about trying to explain to Mum how I felt stuck in my grief for Matty, but at that moment she started telling me with tears in her eyes how proud she was of how I'd coped, how proud Dad was that I was well and happy and living in America, how he talked all the time about my novel, how he was convinced I would be on *Desert Island Discs* one day, how he loved John almost as a son, how it made her so happy that he was happy and how wonderful it was that the family was moving in a positive direction. After all that I didn't have it in me to disillusion her. I nodded and smiled. She and Dad seemed to be getting over everything that had happened to us, and it felt cruel to make them talk about Matty. I didn't want to bring them down by referring to those hard times.

When we moved back to London in the summer of 2002, John threw himself into work and I ricocheted between refusing to leave the house and going on benders for several days. One day John came home with a Caterham 7, a sports car that he'd been given the use of for the weekend as some sort of bonus.

'Get dressed,' he said, 'I want to take you for a drive.'

I could see he was proud of himself and I didn't want to be mean, but I hated the thought of getting in it. However, I decided to make an effort and cleaned my teeth and put on some clothes and even some lipstick. I knew it was a terrible mistake as soon as we set off. The seats were low down and I was far too close to the road. I couldn't stop thinking of Matty, of the horseshoe-shaped scar on his head, of metal staples punctuating shaved scalp, and I started to shake. I tried to do my breathing exercises, but as John was revving the engine, tears were running down my cheeks. We were going round a roundabout when he looked at me.

'What is it?' He had to shout over the noise of the engine.

'I want to go home.'

He drove us back. I got out of the car, went straight to bed and pulled the duvet over my head.

Later, John came and stood in the doorway to the bedroom. 'I feel like I can't get it right with you any more. Everything I do is wrong,' he said.

I didn't reply, and after a while he went away. I thought how once he would have known that I'd be frightened to drive so fast in a stripped-back car and would have cared more about looking after me than trying to have a good time. But I also thought that he deserved to come home to a girl who would enjoy the fruits of his labours, a girl who would cry 'yippee' and jump into the seat next to him, lavishing him with admiring looks. He was worthy of a fully functioning wife, and I was not that wife.

THE LAST REFUGE OF THE
DIRECTIONLESS

Less than three years after we had married, John and I decided to split up. We'd always agreed to have children when I was thirty, and as that birthday approached I knew it was impossible. I was hardly capable of looking after myself, and continually had dreams where I had a baby but got drunk and forgot about it or left it in the back of a taxi. I didn't know what my future held, but I realized I was going to have to work it out alone.

Our separation was amicable. We were full of love for each other, just not the right kind any more. I'd been behaving like John's depressed sister for years, so it was easy to transition to a sibling-style friendship.

I didn't tell my parents. After a few more violent incidents in the pub, they'd decided enough was enough and had found a manager for it so they could retire down to Cornwall. They lived in the house Mum had grown up in, a beautiful granite cottage in Ponsanooth that had once been a council house. My parents had given my grandparents the money to buy it and had then inherited it when they died. They lived a quiet life, sailing and walking the coastal paths near where they first met. I didn't want to be a burden to them, so I only called when I knew I could sound cheerful. They didn't know anything about my struggles and thought I was happily settled with John, living a glamorous jet-setting life.

One day, Mum phoned to say they wanted to go away somewhere warm for a month in the winter as Dad's chest was playing up, thanks to various respiratory problems he had from all the years working underground around coal dust. She wanted to know if we would be able to look after their cat.

For a moment I considered continuing the deceit. I'd been living in a tiny rented room on the top floor of a house in Parson's Green in London for a few months by now. Maybe I could get John to look after the cat by himself. But it didn't seem fair not to tell Mum the truth.

I didn't do a good job of explaining because I didn't know what to say. I could hear she was shocked and I knew Dad would be disappointed. I'd tried to be happy so they wouldn't have to worry about me, but I just couldn't fake it any more.

I suppose our family was a bit like a car. When all four wheels were in place, we drove along for miles very happily. Then Matty's wheel got punctured and the rest of us compensated to keep him going. But now Matty's wheel was gone, my parents were still rolling along up front, and I was a problem wheel, half flat and no longer balanced by my brother, just scraping along the road.

I needed to get a job but there were great gaping holes in my CV. I couldn't bear the thought of having to explain about Matty, so I tried to fudge it to extend the period I'd been unable to work due to travelling with John. I went to a couple of recruitment agencies but could see they weren't impressed. I didn't present myself well, wasn't qualified for anything, and no one liked that I hadn't worked for so long.

The only thing I was good at was reading, and the only thing I knew about was bookshops, as I'd sat around in them all over the world, so I decided to fill out lots of online applications for all the shops I'd heard of; but got no response. Then, someone told me of Harrods' book department, so I borrowed a suit from Sophie and went down to Knightsbridge to try to speak to the manager. When I got there I saw it was a Waterstone's. I especially liked their shops – I had once nearly got locked into the one in Piccadilly when I'd wandered off in the wrong direction after coming out of the bar on the top floor.

'Have you got a CV?' the manager asked.

I handed it over. 'It's awful,' I said. 'Full of holes, but I love books and I promise I'll be really nice to your customers.'

He told me to come back the next day for an interview, and when I did, he offered me the job, starting immediately. That's it, I thought, I'll work in a bookshop and write my novel.

It was a shock at first – much harder work than I'd imagined. Many of the customers were rude, and my feet and my back ached. After a few terrifying days during which I realized that I was nowhere near as well-read as I'd thought, and that I knew nothing about anything – Madeira was owned by Portugal? – it all clicked into place, and I felt a joy at discovering I was a good bookseller. I swelled with an emerging professional pride that I had found a place for me to be.

I thought up novel plots in my head as I shelved books, but I never got much further than that. There were enough books in the world already; nobody needed me to add to the pile. I had very little money and lived off bread and Cup a Soup for the last ten days of every month, but the upside was that I could read for free because publishers sent us advance copies of new books. I got through a book a day, sometimes two or more if it was one of my days off.

The best thing was talking to strangers about books, and I built up a group of customers who would seek me out for recommendations. There was one sweet, posh, elderly lady who would arrive in the department, lean her walking stick against the desk, and demand, 'Where's the girl who reads?'

I made lots of good friends at Harrods and learned about their lives as we manned the front desk together. There was an art to this: we couldn't obviously face each other, but would stand shoulder to shoulder, each scanning the room for customers as we swapped secrets in discreetly low sideways voices. I read *Intimacy* by Hanif Kureishi, in which he describes teaching English as a foreign language as the last refuge of the directionless. I told my bookseller friends about it, and we all laughed at the realization that lots of us aspired to teach English as a foreign language. Many of us felt directionless, that we had washed up together for no discernible purpose.

There was a continual carnival atmosphere. We were

next to the pet shop and Christmas World, and there was much mumbling in the staffroom when we realized that the elves from Santa's Grotto got paid more than we did. There was a staff canteen, roof terrace and smoking room up on the top floor, and the posh food from the famous food halls would often be sold cheap upstairs, so sometimes my lunch would be a slice of Beef Wellington or a lobster mousse for a pound.

On Christmas Eve I cried three times on the shop floor when customers were mean to me. I spent Christmas Day – the first since we had separated – with John. He gave me a Tiffany heart necklace. He was so kind. It would be easy in some ways, I thought, to go back to him. I'd no longer feel I needed to have a purpose of my own and could take up following him around the world again, supporting his career and ironing his shirts. But I knew it wasn't the right thing for either of us. He'd started dating and was enjoying himself. I felt no jealousy at all, just wanted him to be happy, and only hoped that whoever he met wouldn't be difficult about him being friends with me. I didn't know what I'd do without him.

As 2003 began, I sank further into a depression. My parents were still upset with me for splitting up with John and for not telling them about it for so long. My thirtieth birthday felt like a slap, a brutal reminder that I'd achieved nothing with my life. It was a cold and rainy day. I had holes in my shop-girl shoes and my feet got wetter and wetter as I walked home from work among the discarded Christmas trees left out in the street to be collected by the council.

I became obsessed with the idea that it would have been so much better for everyone if I'd been knocked over instead of Matty. I'd been much less fit than he was, and smoked, so perhaps I wouldn't have survived the injury and surgery. There would have been no coma, no eight years. Matty would have been better able to cope with loss than me – he wouldn't still be drunkenly droning on and on about it all these years later to anyone who would listen. If it was Matty who had survived, he'd have lived properly, not been stunted like me. He'd be leading a fuller life, be less handicapped by grief and guilt. He would have achieved things, have an important job and be married to a beautiful, intelligent woman who would give my parents the beautiful and intelligent grandchildren they deserved.

I was stuck. I felt guilty that I couldn't get over it, and guilty that I might ever be able to get over it. I took no pleasure in life and embarked on a grim flirtation with the idea of suicide, though I didn't think I could do that to my parents. I fantasized about opportunities for dangerous self-sacrifice, wishing I could run into a burning building to save a child or go to fight in a foreign war. I tried to think of ways in which I could die accidentally, but there didn't seem to be a method that wouldn't inconvenience or distress someone else. I don't think I ever really wanted to be dead, though. I just wanted not to hurt. I wanted to be able to go to sleep for a very long time and then wake up feeling better.

I remember seeing a demonstration of a vacuum packer in a shop around this time. I stood and watched how this machine sucked all the air out of a plastic bag so that clothes could be neatly packed away and not be at risk of being eaten by moths. That's what I need for my heart, I thought. I need to be able to vacuum-pack away my heart, make it tiny and protected and put it in a cupboard or under the bed so I can get it out again and open it when time has passed and it's safe to feel.

There were times when I didn't think I would need to take action to die. That my poor, beleaguered heart might just stop beating. That the effort of pumping sad blood around my sad body might become too much. My heart might literally break, not in a dramatic way, not with any whizz-bangs or jumping off bridges. It might just decide it had had enough.

By then I was frightened of Matty. He used my dreams to reproach and berate me. Often he appeared thin and gaunt in a blue-and-white striped uniform. Once he banged and banged my head on a table, telling me that I should have killed him when I had the chance, and I woke up to find that the banging was happening on the front door of the other top floor flat, that my neighbour's drunken boyfriend, begging to be let in, had provided a soundtrack for my nightmare. I lay there, shaking and smoking and wondering how I would ever get over the fact that I'd wanted my brother to die.

All I ever did, apart from reading, was get drunk and cry about Matty. I resolved to talk no more about him and I locked the story away. I'd reached an age where people asked less about siblings, and when they did I had a prepared answer.

'I had a brother. He died,' I'd say. If people looked like they might ask questions, I'd add, 'It was a long time ago,' and then change the subject to something jollier.

The diaries and notebooks I'd written my novel into when I lived in France were all in two bags under my bed, and one day I dragged them out and threw them into the rubbish bins outside. I felt weighed down by the existence of all those words, all that sadness. I had too much backstory, I decided, and wanted to liberate myself from it.

I tried speed-dating, Internet dating and even answered an ad in *Private Eye* and went out with a man who wanted a mistress. I got asked out by customers a lot and often said yes.

One night John came over for a drink in the Beauchamp, one of our regular pubs. A few of my Harrods friends came along, including Lizzie, a sweet girl from Hebden Bridge who I'd become fond of.

John rang me up the next day. 'How would you feel if I asked Lizzie out?' he asked.

'Fine,' I said. 'But only if your intentions are honourable.'

Luckily, Lizzie liked him, too, and because she'd had the whole story from me before ever meeting him, she understood our friendship. They started seeing each other.

In general, the discipline of work was good for me and the forced routine and contact with the outside world helped me feel less mad. As time went on, I thought that I might not have found *the* way to live, but I had found *a* way to live.

In the summer of 2004 I got a transfer to the brand new

shop about to open on Oxford Street and went to an induction day in the Simpson Room at Waterstone's Piccadilly. As an ice-breaker we had to find out about the person sitting next to us, including the first single they bought, and then introduce them to the rest of the room. Mine was 'Don't You Want Me, Baby' by the Human League, and my neighbour's, a Dutch boy called Erwyn, was 'Pump Up the Jam' by Technotronic. He was tall and shy and had the remnants of a black eye, which he told me he'd got playing squash. I looked at him and thought, If you've ever played squash in your life, my friend, then I'm the Dutchman.

We got to know each other as we worked in the new shop. I looked after events and loved having to organize the huge celebrity book signings. Erwyn was in charge of operations. He was quiet and didn't say very much, but he knew everything, and I was always impressed by how hard he worked. He was very cooperative and would always lend the services of his team to come and move furniture around and shift crash barriers. Once, when a signing was less well attended than we'd hoped, he and all the goods-in boys put on their coats and swelled the queue to a more respectable number.

Several months later, after a drunken snog, I found myself sitting in the Cock Tavern north of Oxford Street explaining why I didn't want to go out with him.

'Work is the only thing in my life that isn't fucked-up,' I said. 'Besides, I don't want to go out with anyone, or get married, or meet anyone's parents, or own property with someone. And I don't want children.'

'We should go out for another drink and discuss it some more,' he said.

So we started going out. He was kind and incurious, he didn't seem very interested in people, preferring animals and birds, and I liked that he didn't ask me a lot of questions about the past. My loneliness lifted. Eventually I moved in with him in Chiswick, and we stopped smoking and spent a lot of time walking along the riverbank and going to Kew Gardens, where he taught me the Dutch words for different types of geese. After a while I decided I'd like him to meet my parents and I told him the very basics about Matty.

'I had a brother and he died,' I said. 'I don't want to talk about it, but I thought you should know before meeting my parents just in case.'

Of course, neither my parents nor I would mention Matty because we never did – we'd stopped talking about him as we found it too distressing. I thought it unlikely that Erwyn would ask any probing questions, but I wanted to make sure.

A few months later we went on holiday down to my parents' house in Cornwall and spent our time cliff-walking and swimming. We were all having breakfast one morning when Lilly, next door's cat, came in and jumped up onto my lap.

'It's been a very sad time for Lilly,' Mum said. 'Her brother Leo was knocked over by a car and she's been all moping and listless.'

'She's a bit more herself now, though,' said Dad, reaching over to stroke under her chin.

'You could have a little chat with her about it,' said Mum. 'You could say "Oh, Lilly, my brother was knocked over by a car and I was sad too."'

It was a rare mention of Matty, but a sweet and safe one, and we all giggled.

'It's taken me a bit longer to get over it, though,' I said.

'That's OK,' said Erwyn. 'Just the difference between cat time and human time.'

I hoped I'd finally achieved a measure of acceptance. That holiday I wrote a short story in which we buried Matty's ashes in the garden. I based it on us, but the burying itself was imaginary as I wasn't sure what had happened to his ashes. I didn't think we'd ever picked up them up from the undertaker, but it was just about possible that we had done and there'd been some kind of ceremony that I'd blocked out or been too drunk to remember. It was also just about possible that my mother would tell me they'd scattered them into the sea years ago but didn't want to bother me about it and I wasn't sure how that would make me feel. So I wrote my story and showed it to my parents. They liked the story, and were happy that I seemed to be getting over it, though they didn't volunteer any information about what had happened to the ashes and I couldn't bring myself to ask.

NEW LIFE

For some years now I'd thought I wouldn't have children. I'd survived losing Matty by the skin of my teeth and was still mired in grief and guilt, so the risk of creating a new life to love seemed too great. How could I survive the loss of anyone else?

Things changed not long after my thirty-fifth birthday. There was no vulgar-sounding tick-tock; I went to a book launch and the author told me about looking down at her grandchild and recognizing her daughter in the new little girl's face. 'I know you,' she said to her. 'I've seen you before.'

In that moment I knew I wanted a child.

It wasn't the plan to name a baby after my brother. I had always thought it a bit mawkish to name a child after a tragically dead loved one, so we went into the scan ready to see Charlotte Rose or Daniel Jan. But the moment the sonographer said we were having a boy – she was from Miami with a light Southern drawl: 'Oh yes, ma'am, he's all man, all right' – I changed my mind.

'Daniel, then,' said Erwyn as we tried to see our baby on the fuzzy screen.

'Actually, I want to call him Matthew,' I said. 'Is that OK?'

'Of course,' he agreed, without hesitation.

Erwyn adapted well to my ever-changing point of view. Soon after that, I asked him what he'd think if I changed my mind about getting married.

'Fine by me,' he said, and a few weeks later we went to Richmond registry office and then to a restaurant overlooking the river with thirty guests. John was a witness and Lizzie did a reading. Sometimes people were confused that I was still close to John. I would simply explain that I saw him as a replacement brother.

Matt was born in the summer of 2009 after an induction that went a bit wrong and ended in an emergency caesarian after hours and hours of painful labour. It was the first time my dad ever read a whole book in a day, as he sat and waited for news in the hospital coffee shop. Erwyn and Mum were both with me, but only one of them could come to surgery and I felt in need of my mother, so she put on the blue scrubs, which rather suited her, and was the first person to hold Matt when he was lifted out of me.

'She is so wonderful, your mother,' whispered the midwife, 'she should have been a doctor.'

When I went back to work after maternity leave, I was determined not to waste my days. I got a new job running a literacy charity called Quick Reads, commissioning short books for less confident adult readers. I was overwhelmed by all the things I didn't know about charities, fundraising and government, but immediately enjoyed spending time with people who couldn't read or write very well and was inspired and humbled by the way they navigated life.

Some time into the job, I went on a visit to Pentonville

prison with Andy McNab, the SAS hero and thriller writer. Andy was recruited into the army from borstal and credited army education with changing his life. 'Everyone fucks up,' he said, to a room full of prisoners. 'It's what you do next that matters.' I felt the hairs stand up on the back of my neck. I knew in that moment that every single one of us wanted to change our lives for the better. I looked around the room. If all these people, most of whom hadn't had my educational advantages or good parenting, could face their demons and get on with life, then maybe I could too.

I started talking to people about my own dad and all his struggles with reading, realizing it made everyone more comfortable with me when I shared his story – more inclined to trust me and know that I wasn't judging them.

'Thanks for telling us about your dad,' said a man at a prison reading group. 'It's amazing that someone who sounds a bit like me could have a daughter who grows up to be someone like you.' I was very moved by this and it made me think how I must appear very different to people from how I felt inside.

Quick Reads was part time, so I got another job writing about books for the *Bookseller* magazine. I used to read it in my breaks in the smoking room at Harrods, and knew that my lonely, younger self would feel pleased at how I'd turned out. I started talking about books on radio and TV and no longer felt directionless or like a fuck-up. People kept telling me how good I was, and after a while I stopped feeling like a fraud or looking over my shoulder to see if they were talking about someone else and learned to accept their compliments. I knew I didn't present a whole picture: I felt like a burlesque dancer using fans and sleight of hand to hide the bits of myself I felt ashamed of. I didn't think anyone would like me if they knew how I really was.

I was still sad, and troubled by the fact that I could be sad when I had so much to make me happy. How could I be sad when my son was so beautiful, when my parents were alive and in good health, when I had fulfilling work to do?

We went to visit Erwyn's beautiful home town of Edam, where it rained non-stop and I felt the black tentacles of depression trying to get a hold on me. I idly clicked a Twitter link and read an article in *Time* magazine called 'Top Ten Comas' and it made me cry for the rest of the holiday. I was distressed by the flippant tone – they placed fictional characters side by side with real tragedies – and by the accompanying images of the blank stares that reminded me of Matty. The thing that most worried me, though, was the entry about someone who magically woke up many years later. That was the stuff of my nightmares.

Back home, I felt empty. I ached all over and was plagued with frequent aggressive headaches. Every day it was a struggle to get out of bed. I felt like I had lead weights strapped to my legs.

I went to the doctor's and was tested for a few things and then remembered how everything that had ever been wrong with me turned out to have a psychological root. So I went to see a therapist. I wanted to know why I was like this. She said she didn't know but I had lots of unprocessed grief, and I spent the best part of a year crying at her for fifty minutes a week. It worked a bit, in that my aches and pains lessened, but I wasn't sure we were getting anywhere.

One day, when I'd exhausted the box of tissues by the chair, the therapist opened the cupboard next to me to get some more and lots of boxes came tumbling out. I laughed and an idea jumped into my head for a story about a therapist at a cash and carry bulk-buying tissues for all her clients to sob into, clients that for some reason she didn't really care about. Then I felt guilty that I had been so easily distracted and realized that I continually played out this thought process. I felt sad about Matty, I distracted myself from it and then felt guilty about being able to take pleasure in something. I remembered the first time I'd laughed after the accident. I was at a friend's house and her boyfriend said something funny.

How can I laugh? I thought. *How can I laugh?*

Sometimes, to relieve the awful tedium of my misery, I tried to make the therapist laugh. I told her little stories from my week that I thought showed I was making progress in not being relentlessly gloomy.

'I can see you're very amusing,' she said, without cracking a smile. 'I can see you are very personable and have learned to use humour as a defence mechanism. You don't need to entertain me.'

'Will I always be this miserable?' I asked her one day when I didn't feel I would ever stop crying.

'Some people have to do a lot of work on themselves,' she told me.

Not long after that I stopped going.

Months passed and I wasn't sure what to do next. Accept that I would always be a bit unhappy? Try not to think about it? Find another therapist? I wasn't relentlessly miserable by any means. I was able to take pleasure in my family, my friends, my work, but there was always an undercurrent, a low-level background noise. I started to think of it as emotional tinnitus.

I'd become better at managing myself. I read books about how to be happy that sometimes helped. I learned to be moderate in my consumption of both news and alcohol. I made gratitude lists that, if I wasn't at too low a point, would work a bit but would occasionally make me feel worse. On the bad days I'd stare at the lists and think how could I have so much to be grateful for and not be able to summon gratitude? My fear was that some day these feelings would rear up without warning and derail me. The tinnitus would become deafening, my ear drums would burst. I'd find myself down at the riverbank with a couple of bottles of sherry and pockets full of stones. I'd end up in a gutter or dead in a ditch.

One day in the supermarket when I was getting out my wallet to pay, Matt said, 'Who's that, Mummy?'

He was sitting in the trolley pointing to the photo I carried of Matty and me when we were children. I didn't know what to say. It had never occurred to me that my own child might at some point ask me the brothers and sisters question and I would have to find the words to explain. I distracted Matt by giving him my bank card to hand over to the cashier, but I knew that I would have to think about how to answer. 'I had a brother. He died,' wasn't going to be enough for my curious boy. And I didn't want Matt to grow up surrounded by secrets.

REASONS TO FEEL GUILTY

'You need to write it down,' said my new friend Tom in a hotel bar in Korea.

We were on a trip with the British Council. It was exciting to be in the land of sweet-potato lattes and green-tea ice cream, and we'd spent all day talking to arts workers, teachers and librarians about the importance of reading for pleasure. On our second bottle of wine, Tom had asked if I was writing anything myself. People often asked me this and I usually brushed it off, but somehow, possibly because we were half a world away from home or just because Tom is the sort of person who invites confidences, I told him about Matty – that I couldn't bring myself to write about him, but nor could I get very far with anything else before he strode into the pages demanding to be heard.

'Just write it down. Start with the funeral. Start with trying not to laugh at the funeral,' he suggested.

The next day Tom gave me a blue notebook he'd bought in a museum shop, and I wrote about the funeral in it on the flight on the way home.

I'd made several attempts over the years when the words were trying to burst out of me, and I'd managed to write about the night of the accident but could never get past the first few days afterwards, because I couldn't bear to think about how our refusal to accept defeat on Matty's behalf had turned into a grim acceptance that he had to die. Every time, I'd simply downed tools when it became too hard. However, now that, through my job, I'd seen how difficult it was for people to move on when they couldn't articulate their experience, had watched people in prison struggle to make sense of their toxic narratives and try to get to grips with their guilt, I decided to try it for myself.

I made a list of all the reasons I felt guilty.

I feel guilty that I wanted my brother to die
I feel guilty that I didn't like looking after him
I feel guilty that I couldn't bear to visit him in the nursing home
I feel guilty that I couldn't hack the last 13 days of his life, that I had to run away and go back to London
I feel guilty about enjoying things
I feel guilty that I can't just enjoy things
I feel guilty for being happy
I feel guilty that I'm not happier
I feel guilty about being depressed
I feel guilty that I have so much when other people have less
I feel guilty when I laugh
I feel guilty when I cry
I feel guilty when I make other people feel bad
I feel guilty that I can't just get over this
I feel guilty that I could ever get over this

That's it, I thought. *That's the problem. All this guilt festers in me like a gigantic boil, full of poison and painful to touch.* Every time I'd tried to lance it, my courage had failed. Now I was determined to see it through.

ASHES TO ASHES

A month later I was sitting in the car park of Yeovil crematorium with my mother. We had a few minutes before it would be time to go in for the funeral service of her cousin, Sue.

I took a deep breath.

'Did we ever do anything with Matty's ashes?' I asked.

'No. We never picked them up,' Mum said. 'Could never face it. They must still be there, at Mr Punton's.'

Mr Punton, the undertaker, owned a DIY shop in Snaith on the corner of the main street, opposite the Bell and Crown, which had a sign with green letters on a cream background. I went over with my dad sometimes when he needed something to help him fix stuff in the pub. I liked the smell of paint, glue and sawdust, the plastic buckets full of different length screws and nails.

As I sat in the car, I pictured a back room with a row of uncollected urns on a special shelf, full of ash, gathering a fine layer of dust. For a fanciful moment I imagined them whispering to each other, like something out of Harry Potter, and hoped Matty had someone interesting to talk to.

'I could write to him if you like,' Mum said slowly. 'Ask if they're still there.'

'We could find out, I suppose,' I said sensibly. 'Maybe they don't keep them forever.'

The air became filled with unspoken questions: Will they have them? What if the undertakers have a ten-year policy before all the ashes go into a common pit? What if we have waited too long? What would we do with them anyway? Throw them into the sea?

We sat in silence. We usually talked about everything, my mother and I – we were always chatting; but this was an area that we feared stepping into.

'I'm trying to write about it all,' I said.

'Is that a good idea? Won't it make you unhappy?'

'It's OK so far,' I said. I didn't want her to worry. 'Have you still got your diaries and the newspaper cuttings?'

'Yes. I kept them just in case you did want to write about it. I always thought you would. Do what you want with them, but be careful of yourself, Ca.' She sighed. 'Please stop if it's too painful.'

We went into the crematorium and cuddled into each other in a pew towards the back of the room. It was a progression for us that we were even at a funeral. For years our only response to death was to run away. We'd offended relatives and friends by not attending funerals, and then being unable to find the words to explain why.

When it was over, we filed out past a lily pond and went on to a chapel service in Montacute, where the minister said, 'This is a sad day, but Sue would not want us to be sad,' and smiled fondly at the little ones who didn't want to sit still. Then to Lower Odcombe village hall, where I watched my son fall in love with one of his cousins, and my mother told me that it was here, at Sue and Len's wedding nearly forty years ago, that I'd taken my first steps. I did some sums and thought, but didn't say, that Matty would have been in her tummy then, bouncing around getting ready to be born the following February. I felt sad, and wished I didn't. Or rather, I wished I could devote all my sadness to Sue and her children. It seemed to be their due. I should have been feeling only sympathy for them, and gratitude that my own mother was here to have conversations with me and that my father was taking pride in his grandson. As ever, I was stuck, marinating in my own sadness.

'Who would have thought the old man would have had so much blood in him,' said Lady Macbeth, driven mad by guilt, in the play I studied at school before any of this happened.

Who would have thought, I often reflected about myself, *that the young girl would have had so many tears in her*.

Back in London, I told a friend who was a bereavement counsellor about the non-collection of the ashes, and she said it was quite common for people not to pick them up, especially after difficult deaths, especially in the case of a child. This was a revelation: I had thought it was our dark and dirty secret. It made me feel better, less alone, to think that other people had difficulty bringing things to a close too.

LEARNING TO FLY

Summer in Cornwall and the sun was shining. My parents were delighted to be spending time with Matt, taking him rock pooling and swimming, making him a swing in the garden. Watching them together, I was struck by the realization that I was re-experiencing the bits of my childhood that I couldn't remember by seeing my parents with my son. Every game, every caress, every joke was a reflection of how it was with me and Matty when we were little.

One afternoon, right up high, Matt let go of the swing and flew off into the bushes. He wasn't hurt.

'What did you do that for?' asked my dad.

'I wanted to see what would happen.'

I held back from telling him off or urging him to be more careful. I never wanted him to feel how scared I was on his behalf.

Matt was less intrepid at Snakes and Ladders and cried when he was dispatched down a very long snake.

'It is disappointing,' Mum said, 'but you just have to carry on and hope to land on another ladder soon.'

The year after Matty's accident had been like a big, cruel game of Snakes and Ladders, except that there were no ladders, only snakes. We plodded along, only ever throwing ones, making tiny bits of progress in physio; and then, every few squares, a snake in the shape of a massive epileptic fit would send him plummeting back to the beginning. Maybe all of life is a bit like Snakes and Ladders, but most of the time you don't have to blindly throw the dice. You can search out the ladders, create coping strategies for the snakes.

After all the years of silence, of finding it too painful to even mention Matty's name, my parents and I had begun to talk about everything. At first we stumbled over the words, fearful, still, of hurting each other, but as we persevered we became less tongue-tied. I admitted how much Matty dominated my thoughts, and that I didn't want them to worry about me but had realized I had to stop hiding it.

I explained how I felt like I was always about to be ambushed by memories. It might be the sight of someone in a wheelchair with the twisted arms and scars that indicate brain surgery. Matt's baby formula reminded me of Ensure, and when John rang me up to boast that his ridiculously enormous new telly was exactly as long as Erwyn, all I could think was that it would be two inches shorter than Matty.

'I wish I could erase those eight years of my life,' I said. I told them that from the ages of seventeen to twenty-five I would rather have not been alive. I didn't think I should have had to bear it. I didn't think anyone should have to bear it. 'I would like to be able to press delete on those years,' I said. Select and delete.

It was such a relief to tell them the truth, and of course they took it all in their stride and jumped into the task of helping me remember everything. We sat in the garden or walked along the seafront in Falmouth, and talked and talked as we'd done on all those walks along the riverbank in Snaith.

I sat in their little sitting room and looked through our photo albums. I found a yellowed newspaper clipping about my dad – 'a young Cork seaman' – saving a life when he was seventeen. He'd been given a certificate from the Royal Humane Society, and I could remember Matty and me taking it into school for show and tell. I looked at my parents' wedding photos. A carefree joy shone out of my dad's twinkling eyes; my mother looked nervous. She was less comfortable being the centre of attention than he was. They both looked so young – but then they were: eighteen and twenty-two. I was there in the photos, too, an unseen tadpole wriggling around in my mother's still flat tummy.

Everyone said it wouldn't last, this marriage between the head girl of the grammar school and the illiterate, tattooed Irishman who had knocked her up. But Mum had fallen for Dad as soon as she'd heard him speak. She had never heard an accent like his before, a lovely, lilting, foreign sound. She was studying *The Tempest* at school and felt like Miranda seeing Ferdinand for the first time: 'Oh brave new world, That has such people in't'. When he had told her of his early life, of the Christmas morning he'd woken up to find his stocking empty, she was determined that his future would be full of love.

When my parents moved back into this house, the house where my mother grew up, and stripped off the layers and layers of wallpaper, they found his name scratched into the wall by her during the decorating she did with her father before leaving home. They left it uncovered and put a frame over it. It looks down on them when they sit on the sofa beneath, over forty years later, still more in love than anyone else I have ever seen.

More albums: photos of Matty and me as chubby-cheeked children being bathed together in the sink of the caravan, opening presents and putting on plays against the orange and brown decor of the seventies. There are photos of one Christmas where I appear to be continually playing a recorder, which must have been a treat for everyone. I found a photo of the record player that was the unfairly blamed culprit in the mystery of the missing words of 'Frosty the Snowman'. There we were with our cousins, Deb, Tadgh and Kevin in Ireland. Tadgh and Kevin were in identical home-made sweaters, and Matty was sticking his tongue out.

We get older. I am transformed from a fat baby to a dreamy, quiet little girl, into a boisterous teenager with Sun-In hair and ill-advised blue eyeliner. I was forever pulling faces, posing, laughing. All that arrogant, unbruised promise. I hated to think how little time there was before my younger self would have all her joyful silliness crushed out of her.

I found it almost as painful to remember how happy we were before the accident as I did to think about what had happened afterwards, and knew that I should try to stop allowing the accident to ruin my memories.

When I got back to London, I only just stopped myself collapsing on the escalator at Piccadilly tube station when a busker played 'Wish You Were Here', and it prompted me to make a playlist of all the songs that reminded me of Matty, which I listened to again and again. It felt like I was reclaiming my family. The Dubliners, ELO, Gerry Rafferty. The first song on the list was 'Mattie's Rag', which Dad always sang to us after being away, or when he came home from a night shift.

I remembered Dad being away for work in Dubai and how powerfully I missed him. I used to get into the cupboard under the stairs and wrap myself up in his coat – a big blue checked woollen thing with a fleecy lining – so that I could smell him.

We were such a happy family.

Not all the memory ambushes were bad. I bought Matt several pairs of new pyjamas, including some in a Superman design with a wonderful detachable cape. As I was helping him put it on, adjusting the Velcro pads, he looked up at me through his eyelashes, slightly shy, and asked, 'I won't be able to actually fly, though, will I, Mummy?'

'No, darling,' I said, and out of nowhere I remembered being with Matty at Almond Tree Avenue and using towels to make wings so that we could practise flying off the sofa. We took it in turns. When Mum asked what we were doing, we told her, 'We're learning to fly.'

So I was learning to fly with my brother when we were probably both not much older than my son. I don't remember how often the flying happened – whether I'm remembering a few minutes, an afternoon, or whether it was a regular game – but I do remember it, and at a time when I thought all my pre-accident memories of my brother had been played to death, it felt like a most precious gift.

THE BOX OF DESPAIR

I retrieved what I thought of as the box of despair from my parents' house and brought it up to London. It sat in the corner of my bedroom for a few weeks as I threw it occasional nervous glances.

Then one morning I woke up and decided to go for it. I spread the contents out on the sofa. First I looked at the diaries my mother had kept in little red notebooks. The opening pages showed me I had wrongly remembered the trip from Pontefract to Leeds on the first night of the accident. I thought I'd been alone in the back seat, whereas in fact my mother had sat with me, trying to console me in an agony of crying.

I found Matty's exam certificates and a card holding the £10 voucher from WHSmith, the prize that I had collected on his behalf along with the trophy when I went to the presentation evening at his school. His school reports told of a bright, inquisitive and easily distracted boy. I read some of his essays, running my fingertips over his handwriting.

I felt again the tragedy of Matty's transformation, the loss of him as a person, but I also felt full of fondness and compassion for everyone involved, including myself. I'd spent so much time stewing in guilt, worrying about the ways in which I had failed Matty and my parents. Perhaps now, I thought, I should try to simply feel sorry for the girl who flits through the pages of her brother's life and death. She was very young, and very hard on herself, and living through a truly awful situation.

As I looked at Matty's beautiful face staring up at me from the newspaper clippings and read the opinion of one of his examining doctors that 'Matthew Mintern is the most severely brain-damaged person that I have ever seen', I considered the other pillar of my guilt: that I should be more over it, that I should be able to count my blessings and get on with life. But as I looked through all the notes and diaries that charted our journey, I saw clearly that it would be impossible to have had a heart and lived through this unscathed, and I felt a growing sense that maybe I could look my guilt in the face and think about being a little less hard on myself in the future.

PROLONGED DISORDERS OF
CONSCIOUSNESS

I wanted to find out what was going on in those cases in the paper where people woke up from a coma after many years, and also whether there had been any medical or legal developments in the years since Matty's accident. I didn't approach it lightly, and was terrified I'd induce the spiralling despair I had felt in Holland on reading the coma article. However, I screwed my courage to the sticking post, and Mum offered to help. It was she who found a recently published report on 'Prolonged disorders of consciousness' from the Royal College of Physicians. I read it with a growing sense of delighted relief.

> The legal precedent for withdrawal of CANH [Clinically Assisted Nutrition and Hydration] in VS [vegetative state] was set in 1993 in the case of Anthony Bland, who sustained catastrophic anoxic brain injury in the 1989 Hillsborough disaster. As a result of that judgement, the legal position is that it is lawful to withdraw CANH from a patient who is in VS. Since then, over 40 applications have been made to the Court of Protection to

withdraw CANH in patients in permanent VS, and the required declarations have been granted.

Once it is known that a patient is in permanent VS, the Court accepts that further treatment is futile. It is not only appropriate but necessary to consider withdrawal of all life-sustaining treatments, including CANH. Indeed, to continue to deliver treatment that prolongs their life in that condition in the absence of a reasonable belief that treatment is in the patient's best interests may be regarded as an assault.

I fell in love with that phrase: 'not only appropriate but necessary'. I felt the burden of responsibility shift.

Many families will have been informed during the early acute stage of injury that the patient is unlikely to survive. Once the patient has survived, apparently against all odds, miracles may seem not only possible but likely, and family members may see their loved one as a 'fighter' with a determination to recover which will overcome physiological obstacles.

Yes! I remembered our absolute conviction that Matty's fitness and determination on the football field would translate into recovery.

However, with hindsight, efforts to save their loved one's life may be viewed with regret. One family member said: 'Would that they hadn't got to Charlie in time to resuscitate him – knowing now what I didn't know then.'

Even those who fight for all active measures in the early months or years may change their minds about the appropriate course of action in the future.

Yes and yes. I remembered Killingbeck and the heroic attempts to cure the lung infection that could so easily have been allowed to develop into pneumonia, those hard years of gradually coming to see the futility of our efforts to prolong Matty's life.

On occasions, the initiation (and cost) of bringing applications to the Court has been left to the family. The GDG believes this is wrong. The legal costs of the Court application should be borne by the responsible public body, and the onus for initiating the application should lie with the treating clinical organisation or those who commission the care.

We all felt too responsible. Too much like it was us giving up. I had started to feel like a murderer.

Challenges for end-of-life care and place of death

Patients dying in VS pose a number of challenges for management which include the following:

The process of dying is often prolonged and timing of death difficult to anticipate.

Patients with profound brain injury typically have complex spasticity and involuntary movements requiring skilled postural handling techniques and specialist equipment often not available in standard hospice settings.

Patients dying in VS frequently exhibit signs of 'physiological distress' (see below), which may give the appearance of suffering even when the patient him/herself is unaware. Such signs are distressing for family and care staff to witness.

Managing end-of-life care in this difficult situation often challenges care staff to their limits. For all these reasons, end-of-life care for patients with VS or MCS requires a team-based approach with close coordination between specialists in palliative care and neurodisability management. The combined skills of both specialties are required to optimize medication, to support distressed family members, and also to support the care team.

I read through the report again and again and found it very comforting. There was a lot about the burden on relatives that made such brilliant sense. I felt less like a weed when I read about how clinicians have to be specially trained, that withdrawal is distressing for everyone, that counselling programmes should be in place. I wasn't cross – I didn't think it was anyone's fault – but I hoped that if it happened now it wouldn't unfold for others the way it did for us. It really shouldn't have been Mum and Dad alone in the bungalow with a supply of diazepam suppositories.

In all the medical reports about Matty in the box of despair there are occasional mentions of me, of my psychological problems, of my state of mind, of how I was finding his condition difficult to come to terms with. Reading this report, I realized that there was nothing unusual in that, there was nothing unusual about me, there was nothing unusual about my family, except our exposure to a desperately cruel and unusual situation.

AN IMPERFECT WORLD

Feeling buoyant after the success of my research, I decided to revisit the hospital in Leeds as it was the site of so much of my story. I emailed the infirmary, who said that a chaplain would show me round.

Everything looked different when I got off the train. It could have been anywhere. I bought a coffee, fumbling over the change with nervous fingers. Only when I reached the town hall with its giant outdoor chessboard was I in familiar territory.

I'd thought a lot about the chapel over the years, about the night I'd prayed there after leaving Matty's bedside. In my mind I was expecting a carefully non-denominational wooden box, underground and airless. When I got there, I stared at the stained-glass window and the altar and was disorientated to realize I'd misremembered it.

Jane, the chaplain, exuded practical kindness and I felt I was in the hands of an expert. She had brought me a booklet about the history of the chapel and pointed out the lurid green face of the ill person depicted in the stained glass. I learned that I wouldn't be able to wander into the chapel late at night now. It closes at 9.30 p.m. because they had too many problems with syringes behind the altar. I'd asked if I could see one of the overnight bedrooms for relatives, wondering if the tiny white room was as I'd remembered, but they are long gone too. In front of the prayer tree, reading the supplications of those in agonies of worry for their loved ones, I wished I could pray for them. *I hope things work out*, I said in my head, *or if they don't, I hope the aftermath is not too brutal; that it is not as long as it has been for me.*

Jane told me about the baby memorial service they hold each year before Christmas. One year four friends, women in their eighties, came after seeing the ad in the local paper. They'd all lost a baby and had never spoken about it to each other, or anyone, until the ad in the paper had prompted them to make a group expedition, each of them holding a rose, each of them crying for a lost baby. I was struck by the gap, the huge length of time over which they had bottled up their own toxic narratives. Fifty, sixty years, probably. How long does grief last?

Jane and I had discussed by email that I wouldn't be able to see the ICU and that the other wards had all moved, but she took me to see an old-style ward that would have been similar to the one Matty was on, and a new-style ward where an adult male patient who had had neurosurgery would now be transferred to after intensive care.

There was a fresh, fruity smell in the air not dissimilar to the mango-scented preventative nit spray I combed through Matt's hair every morning. We walked through the wards and on past the garden where we'd wheel Matty on fine days, and on again to the canteen, which was transformed. But everything was different now. There was a roof terrace. And a Costa.

We stood and chatted in the corner of the canteen, which had been renamed the Food Court.

'Can I ask you a theological question?' I said to Jane.

'Oh, go on then.' She laughed.

'Where do you think the soul is, in a very brain-damaged person?'

I had worried about this a lot over the years. What would a religious person think about where Matty's soul was and at what point it left his body?

'I believe in an all-loving God holding our souls safe. It's an imperfect world, though, I know that.'

I wasn't sure I understood, but I liked Jane. We talked about the benefits of faith, about the difficulties of not knowing what to believe when you don't believe.

Then I thanked her, left the infirmary and walked back down past the chessboards to the train station.

On the train back to London, I thought about why revisiting the hospital was so much less distressing than I'd feared, and realized that I'd braced myself to cope with the sight of a patient who would remind me of Matty. I didn't need to, because we didn't see anyone in his condition. That's how rare it was.

According to the report on 'Prolonged disorders of consciousness', there had been forty successful applications for withdrawal of clinically assisted nutrition and hydration since the case of Tony Bland in 1993. Someone was far more likely to have won the lottery than they were to have died by withdrawal. I wondered how the stats stacked up: how many people had brain surgery after an accident, how many survived, how many got some kind of meaningful life back, how many were left with severe neurological deficits, how many were left in PVS.

Did anyone get fully better? Was there ever any real possibility that Matty would have recovered anything of his real self? I thought of all those cases you read about in newspapers where people magically wake up, but realized that I didn't remember one single real example of anyone being left in anything other than a pitiful situation. No one had ever said to us, 'Oh, you need to meet Jamie/Michael/Bob – in a coma for three weeks and then PVS for a couple of years but now skipping around like a good 'un.' Nothing like that ever happened.

I needed to find some proper answers, and the next day I went back to the report, hoping I'd be able to find someone involved who might talk to me. Looking at the list of authors, I saw that Jenny Kitzinger was both a professor at Cardiff University and an insider researcher; her sister had been in a minimally conscious state after a road accident. Knowing that she too had witnessed the destruction of a sibling helped me feel brave enough to email her to ask if there were any statistics on likely outcomes following head trauma and surgery. Jenny emailed straight back offering to chat, and I tapped out her number with shaking hands. As we talked, she told me reliable statistics were hard to come by, but it was estimated that 6,000 people in the UK were in VS. Her own research was focused on collecting experiences of relatives of someone with a brain injury to share with medical professionals and practitioners and other families. After we'd been on the phone for over an hour, Jenny asked how I'd feel about being interviewed on film for her project. I agreed immediately. She was kind and knowledgeable and I was full of relief that I no longer felt so alone.

'Can I ask you something else?' I said, my heart thudding.

'Of course.'

'I worry about this a lot. I know deep down that Matty was wrecked, his brain was destroyed, but what is happening in those cases where people wake up from comas after several years? I don't understand it.'

'Well,' said Jenny, 'miracle stories do float about, but in general the person will have been less ill than reported and the recovery will be less dramatic than reported. Newspapers like a good story, don't they?'

It was a revelation. But, I realized, I should have known. The same thing had happened to us when Matty's exam results were supposed to have triggered him waking up and smiling. Our story too had contributed to the false idea that a serious head injury can be fixed with a bit of good news.

A few weeks later I sat in Jenny's house in Cardiff and looked out over Penarth Bay as she filmed me crying my way through the whole story. I was in tears telling her about the journey in the ambulance.

'I didn't think I'd start crying this early. This isn't even the bad bit. I find talking about the accident quite easy, because in comparison to what came later it's not particularly distressing.'

'What do you mean?'

'It's such a tiny part of the whole. I accumulated all this knowledge I didn't want after Matty was knocked down. That first night I learned how it feels when the person you love most is close to death. It was rough at the time, but it doesn't even make the Top Ten of the worst moments.'

I talked about the erosion of hope, my guilt at wishing for Matty to die.

'I feel damaged by the fact that I wanted his death. It's really bad for your soul somehow, it goes against what you think you should be like and what you think you should want as a good person.'

Jenny asked whether I thought my parents should feel guilt too.

I was aghast. 'No, of course not. Of course I don't.'

'Then why should you?'

In the silence that followed I felt my world shift. Yes, why should I?

I asked about whether other people would have known how little hope there was. Jenny thought that when the surgeon said he had saved Matty's life but didn't know if it was the right thing to do, he would have had a pretty good idea that the chances of a full recovery were already extremely low. And it narrowed considerably over the next few weeks and months. After a year with no responses Matty should have been defined as being in a permanent vegetative state. Jenny asked whether anyone had ever told us this.

'No, but we might not have been receptive to that conversation. Mum remembers the physio saying to her, "We're not winning." That was his expression. I think we probably didn't want to be told.'

Every so often we'd take a break and Jenny would make us coffee. I'd nibble at one of her home-made biscuits and look out at the boats crossing the bay before sitting back down on the sofa and waiting for her to switch the camera on again.

We talked about the report and how I had found solace in knowing that other families have had similar experiences to ours.

'The report showed me that people change their minds – move from being convinced there's a future to wanting their relative to die. It helped me to see that I behaved like anyone would in that situation, because there's no road map for it.'

Jenny told me that there are people out there who have played my role in this process and feel proud. I think I might have felt proud if it had happened sooner. I know that when I first wanted us to consider withdrawal I was focused on what was best for Matty. The problem was, it dragged on so long that by the time it came to it, I desperately wanted it for me, too, and that was confusing.

Jenny asked why it mattered to continue to provide Matty with excellent, superior care, even when we knew he had no awareness.

'There's a difference between thinking someone doesn't hear the music and stopping playing it for them. Even if you don't think someone can feel pain, you don't want them to get bedsores. Even if you don't think somebody is aware of their circumstances, you don't want them to have dirty hair. I knew that as long as Matty's body remained alive, I would feel tortured about what was happening to him. And I would need to care about what was happening to his body, and I would need to care about who was washing his hair, and I would need to know that people were not being unkind to him, and I would need to know that he was being looked after, even if I couldn't bear to do it myself; even thinking he wouldn't know about it.'

We talked about my own end-of-life wishes.

'I wouldn't want to be kept alive with a headache, frankly,' I said, laughing. 'I'm not quite saying that if I stubbed my toe I'd want someone to hit me over the head with a hammer to put me out of my misery, but it's not far off.'

'What advice would you give?' asked Jenny. 'If you could say one thing to families at the start of this journey, what would it be?'

It was so horrible to think of anyone being subjected to any of this that I struggled to find an answer to her question. But eventually I said, 'Treat yourselves and each other with kindness and compassion. That's what I'd say.'

'Do you think you might be able to take a bit of that advice yourself?'

I looked at Jenny's kind face. I thought about her and all the other relatives. All of us dealing with a situation that was just too hard to bear. I thought of my parents, how fortunate I was to be so well loved. I thought of my little boy. When I was heavily pregnant I spent a lot of time in Chiswick library. There was a bench outside which bore a dedication: 'For my mother, a woman of courage and compassion.' I'd often sit on the bench looking at the plaque and wishing I knew the story behind it. I'd rest my hands on my tummy, feel Matt move inside me, wonder how I could ever measure up.

Now I think maybe I did, maybe I have. Maybe I was already a woman of courage and compassion. Maybe I could learn to treat myself with the kindness I'd feel for someone else in my situation.

'I think so, yes,' I said to Jenny.

Jenny drove me to the station, and on the way back to London I stared at my tear-stained, puffed-up reflection and thought about all the other times I'd seen my grief-laden face in train windows. I realized that I no longer wanted to press delete on those eight years. Matty had needed me. Our parents had needed me. We carried out the hardest of duties in the cruellest of circumstances. 'This is our last act of love for Matty,' Mum had said in her affidavit, and she was right. I'd forgotten over the years how it would have been easier not to do it. It would have been easier to abandon Matty and never face that tough decision, but we did the right thing.

A few weeks later, Jenny sent me a link so that I could preview the website my interview clips would appear on. I dreaded watching them, but as I cried my way through, I began to feel admiration and respect for this girl, this woman, trying so hard to find words for the unsayable. She didn't look flaky or mad. She looked intelligent, thoughtful, brave. I'd grown so used to thinking of my experience of what happened to Matty as a millstone that weighed me down, as a toxic narrative I couldn't express, that it was strange to find that my experience had value.

Now I could see myself in a wider context. I was . . . I don't really want to say 'a victim', but 'a by-product' of a wider societal problem – that we don't know how to deal with the shades of grey that now exist around life and death. We don't know what to do with the unsuccessful output of the surgeon's scalpel. Reading and seeing the testimony of the other relatives, I was fascinated that they thought the same way I do, often using the same language. This isn't group-think, because no one is yet talking openly with each other about this. We've arrived at certain thoughts because of our individual but shared experience. I watched a man say almost exactly what I had once said, that we extend more courtesy to serial killers on death row than we do to our nearly dead. There was a lot of talk about pets, how it's better to be a poorly animal than a poorly person. I remembered taking Sophie's cat Minnie to the vet for her final journey, her sweet truncated last miaow. There are kinder ways to bring life to an end than starving someone to death.

A few nights later, I dreamt of Matty. He did not look like a person with a damaged brain. His face was animated, though old and etched with lines. He had that look you see in middle-aged men who are in prison, or homeless, or addicts. It's a greyish, weary look that speaks of endurance and suffering and of subjecting the body to excess. Back in Snaith, in the pub, we'd have described such a look by saying, 'you can tell he had a big paper round', and everyone would have laughed, while acknowledging that some have greater burdens to bear than others. Often, in such faces, eyes that have borne too much witness are cast down and reluctant to be seen and read.

But in my dream, my still handsome brother looks at me out of his tired, kind eyes, and forms his thin, pale lips into a smile. 'I'm glad you did it,' he says. 'Thank you for doing it.'

I stroke his face, run my fingertips gently over the crow's feet cut around his slate-blue eyes, and then lay my palm flat against his beautiful face.

'My dear,' I say, 'I'm so sorry. I'm so very, very sorry.'

'I know,' he says, letting his face rest against my hand. 'I know.'

CALLING TIME

Over the last couple of years, I've written this story into notebooks and laptops, on planes, trains and in motorway service stations. I've dropped Matt at school and gone round the corner to the Café Rouge that overlooks the Thames, where I have a regular table next to a power socket. I found the same disposable fountain pens full of purple ink, and always have several about me; on my desk, in my pockets or in my bag. I've thought it all out while walking across London from meeting to meeting. I've learned to love the river; I worry less that I might throw myself into it. I walk across all the bridges, and like to stop halfway, looking down to St Paul's, up to the Palace of Westminster.

I feel lucky to be alive in my time. I don't limp, I stride. Sometimes I almost think I'm floating, that my feet aren't touching the ground, but I know they are because I can hear the confident click-clack of my boots. When it's going well, I can write straight onto my phone, standing up on a packed tube. When I'm questioning the wisdom of doing it at all, I sit sullenly in front of my laptop watching my fingers bleed into the keyboard. There are times when it has felt like an exercise in self-harm, but I've trusted in my determination to lance the boil and I do now think that the poison has been drained away.

Matty's ashes are safe at the undertaker's – they have some dating back fifty years – and one day I'll pick them up from Yorkshire, but I'm not quite ready yet. What's the rush? We are still at the grief party, after all. A place where the clocks have no rules, where the bar is always open. A place that you get a pass from, after a while. A stamp on your hand that allows you in and out, that lets you come and go, though not quite as you please. The only mistake, on being allowed out of the party, is thinking that you won't be back.

Grief is not linear. If you could plot it on a graph, you wouldn't see a continuous upward gradient from tragedy to recovery but a sharp set of zigzags. It's tempting to think that collecting Matty's ashes, doing something with them, will feel like an ending, but I'm not sure the gaping hole where I long for my brother to be will feel much less vast, that the edges of that gaping hole will feel less ragged. Sometimes an absence can become as significant in our lives as a presence.

I remember one of our customers in the pub had a tear-drop tattooed under her eye in honour of her dead brother. I don't want a tattooed teardrop, but that's how I feel. Victorians wore mourning brooches. I don't want to be wearing something full of Matty's dead hair, but I'd almost like a visible sign. A mourning ribbon. Black gloves. I don't think I will ever not be sad about this.

But there is so much to be thankful for. The box of despair is unpacked and distilled into these pages. I now think of myself as carrying a rucksack of grief. In some ways it is my ballast. I'm used to it. Occasionally it is so heavy that I'm not sure I can continue carrying it, but most of the time it's bearable and some days I hardly notice it at all. I have to trust that the me without the rucksack – or with a lighter load – would not float away. That if I succeed in putting down my burden, there will be something else there. That I am not just the sister of Coma Boy.

I've learned that almost everyone has a rucksack. The world is full of people carrying around a toxic narrative, pulled down by a sadness or a grief that they don't know how to share, and all of us are hiding it from each other. I used to bury myself in books about grief, but now I talk to real people about it too. One of the problems of being over-dependent on books is that I crave the degree of narrative resolution that you find in novels. Talking more to real people has helped me to see life as the glorious, unshaped mess that it is. Things won't fit, won't behave, won't allow themselves to be finished, finite, completed.

When I started writing this, I thought I just (just!) had to force myself to sit down and write down what I knew. I would order my thoughts, admit my fears, look my guilt in the face. I've done all that, but as time has gone on, what I think about what happened has changed.

I've told the truth as I see it and remember it. I've been a bit light on the details, especially around my own maddery, which is a word I've pinched from Marian Keyes. And boyfriends! I've left out significant others and insignificant others, but there were a lot of them. There were men who had a bit of a thing for damaged girls, and men who thought

I should just get over it. For years I left a trail of broken glass wherever I walked. I'm not proud of lots of things I did in my quest to distract myself from my grief. I'm not proud of my excesses, though I have survived, and was always fortunate in the kindness of strangers and the forgiveness of my friends.

These days, I'm happy to be my real and full self in front of people and I'm less frightened of love. I'm allowing myself to love Matt more, to let him love me.

'When will you die, Mummy?' he asked the other day.

'I don't know, darling, nobody knows.'

'It won't be till I'm a grown-up, though, will it?'

'I hope not, but no one can say for sure.'

'I don't want you to die, Mummy.'

'I know, darling. It's so sad when people die. But they do.'

Grief is the price we pay for love. It is, we have to believe, better to have loved and lost than never to have loved at all. I had a brother. I learned about love by loving him. He had the first bits of my heart. He died.

'It's a design fault, surely?' I said to my mother once. 'It can't be right that as humans we are so maimed by the loss of each other when we are so fragile.'

'Well, we were designed before the internal combustion engine, weren't we?' she replied. 'Both physically and emotionally. If we were being designed now we would be built with harder heads and harder hearts.'

There is no longer a family conspiracy of silence about Matty. My parents and I talk about him, and what happened after the accident, a lot. My mother said that she didn't want to talk to me too much about her grief for Matty because she didn't want me to feel that I wasn't enough. She also thinks I'm wrong to think of myself as second best, as the weaker sibling. She pointed out that people would have said just as many nice things about me, had I been knocked over; they would just have been different. Instead of telling the nurses that I could do a hundred press-ups at a time, they would have been talking about how full of life and love I was, how I could make everyone laugh and feel happy. She reminded me that, in the years before I became grief-dumb, people used to say that there was no need for me to kiss the Blarney stone, I'd been born with the gift of the gab, I could charm the birds from the trees.

She now knows my secret theory that it would have been better for everyone if I'd been knocked over instead, and she doesn't agree.

'I don't think I'd have survived without you,' she says. 'Matty could never have done what you did. He was lovely, so lovely, but he never had the love in him that you have. He couldn't have kept the family together like you have. He'd have been upset, very upset, and probably very inventive at the early stages of rehab, but pretty soon he'd have been off. He wouldn't have wanted to hang around and watch his dad cry, watch my false hopes, wouldn't have had a drop of your sensitivity. I don't know what we would have done without you every step of the way. We needed you. We needed you for the survival of the family.'

Our family does now function again. We have remade ourselves into a three-wheeled car, a Robin Reliant. We'll never have the shining splendour of our top-of-the-range pre-accident model, but we drive along pretty well. I no longer feel like a broken wheel and nor do I feel a weight of expectation. I'm no longer trying to be everything – I'm just being me, and that's pretty good.

And there are no secrets. One afternoon last summer, out in the garden at Ponsanooth, my dad told the story of a disastrous family trip to Helston boating pond with my granny. It was when Matty and I were about six and seven. Dad was hungover and it was a Sunday in the days when pubs shut at 2.30. He was hoping to slope off for a livener but could see the chance slipping away. Giving up on it, he agreed to take Matty out on the pond. There were normal rowing boats, but Matty had set his heart on a Canadian canoe.

'It doesn't look that stable to me, Matty,' Dad said, rocking it from side to side with his hand.

'It'll be fine, Dad,' Matty said, jumping in and picking up the oars.

A few minutes later they capsized, Matty swam away for dear life, and Dad stood up and realized they were only in a foot or so of water.

Granny was on the bank saying, 'That's my son-in-law,' and Mum was telling her to shut up.

We were all in hoots at the story. Matt was listening intently, taking it all in. Later, he asked, 'Was there another boy called Matthew?'

'Yes, darling, there was. There was another boy called Matthew.'

And I told him a version of the story that his four-year-old mind could grasp. He knows I had a brother who died when he was knocked over by a car. He knows it made me very sad.

I had a brother, he died. I could endlessly elaborate on that sentence, but perhaps that's enough for now.

I think a lot about the pub, about how we enjoyed ringing the big bell for last orders on busy nights and then calling time after a last flurry of ones for the road. Is that what I've done, here? I've rung for last orders on all my guilt and now I'm ready to call time on it.

I know I'm damaged. As I've walked through fire, bits of me have burnt off – but I accept that. I've come across a new word. Kintsugi is a Japanese style of ceramics where broken crockery is mended in an intentionally obvious way. Rather than try to hide the crack, it is filled in with gold and the breakage becomes a part of the object's story. I love this idea.

I think how I am often drawn to broken people and find them beautiful. I have decided that I can stop yearning to be fixed or trying to hide the scars: I can decide to think of my brokenness as an integral and even beautiful part of me. I've gathered up all my scattered selves and don't feel fragmented any more.

Perhaps the most miraculous thing is that I no longer feel mad or in need of a diagnosis or a magic medicine. The other day Matt, now five and enjoying Maths at school, announced that he was counting to infinity. That's it, I thought. My sadness is infinite. I feel sad whenever I think about it. I cry whenever I think about it. But I no longer expect that my tears will come to an end. I am no longer surprised that my reservoir of grief is so full and refillable. Because I am no longer surprised, I am much better able to live with it. I weave it into my days. I can cry and laugh at the same time.

I dream of Matty. He's there at the bunjee-jumping place in France, sitting next to the camera. He's grinning back at me, willing me to jump, willing me to fly safely and bounce back.

Somewhere along the way, my grief story became a love story. I have worked out that the only way to be alive in the world is to carry out acts of love and hope for the best.

Dear Matty,

My dear, my dear,

I've been thinking about Blackadder. *Do you remember
how we loved it and used to quote it at each other all
the time? I was remembering the bit in* Blackadder Goes
Forth *where they have been captured by the Germans and
are warned about what to expect. A fate worse than death,
they are told, in a silly German accent. And do not try to
escape or you will suffer even worse. Even verse.*

*'A fate worse than a fate worse than death?' says
Blackadder with his famous raised eyebrow. How we
laughed. You were so funny. I'm sorry I lost sight of that.
I think about it a lot at the moment. I remember you
dancing around wearing the traffic cone, hitting me on
the forehead with a spoon. And* The Young Ones.
We'd sidle up to each other:

'You dancing?'

'You asking?'

'Yes.'

'Well, piss off.'

*My dear, my dear, what I wanted to say, really, was that
I have realized that it could have been worse. You suffered*

a fate worse than a fate worse than death, but it did come to an end for you and there was a legal solution. Other people who are a tiny bit 'better' are worse off in that there is no legal end to their half-lives.

I've worried and worried over the years about what an unnatural thing it is to desire and bring about the death of a loved one. How could I have wanted you to die when I loved you so much? But I see now that it is a question of cause and effect and that desiring death is merely the effect. The cause is that we are unnaturally able to prolong life and that no one has much of an idea or plan about what should happen when life-saving interventions and neurosurgery lead to a horrible outcome. That's why people like me are made to feel like murderers. It shouldn't happen. I nearly went doolally. Want some more Blackadder? I was ready to put my underpants on my head and a couple of pencils up my nose and be of no use to anyone.

My little boy Matt reminds me of you. I can see he'll grow into the things you liked: Meccano, technical Lego, science experiments. He loves Star Wars. We watch it again and again, and he said the other day that he thought Darth Vader would have been a nicer boy if he'd had a mummy and daddy to look after him, which is both cute and true. We were lucky to have our parents. Do you remember how you always wanted Mum to do my hair like Princess Leia? I carry a photo of us around in my wallet. We are maybe seven and eight. My hair is in plaits and you have your hand curled around one of them.

Matt would have loved the garage at the pub. I wish we could time-travel and take him to it before it was knocked down to make room for the bungalow. He'd be drawn to the disused motorbikes, tool boxes and experiments. I've no idea what you were doing in there. I wouldn't have been interested in what you were trying to find out; I only ever cared about understanding how people work. You and him, though — I wish I could see you with your heads together as he asked questions you'd know the answer to. I wish I could see you lift him up in your arms and dangle him over the inspection pit. I can almost hear the excited shrieking.

All being well, I have another eleven years of watching Matt grow up to be the age you reached, and then he'll pass you by, pass us by. In some ways, I think of us both as frozen in time in your garage or sprawled on your bedroom floor listening to music. I left a bit of myself there, though I, of course, did get to grow up, did get to carry on in the world, which has not always felt like the blessing it should have. I'm listening to Brothers in Arms *by Dire Straits as I write this. I remember us lying on the bank at Granny's in Ponsanooth in the sunshine as it floated out of the window. We were still some time away then from your destruction. From me witnessing your suffering.*

When I went to Cardiff and was interviewed about everything that happened to you, I talked about how insane it felt for me to ever complain about anything when you were as damaged as it was possible to be without being dead. It made me think again about when I stopped talking to you. The thing was, I couldn't tell you the truth. I always talked to you as though you understood everything I said, so I couldn't tell you how terrible it was to be without you. I told you happy stories and jokes. I didn't tell you about lying drunk and sobbing on toilet floors at other people's birthday parties. I couldn't talk to you about how it felt to gradually realize that you weren't getting better and you weren't going to get better. I didn't tell you that I didn't want to go on without you. I didn't stop talking to you for years, but I censored myself from the very early days. I couldn't tell you the truth about what was happening to you, or about what was happening to me without you.

I'm enjoying writing to you. I feel a bit like Harry Potter sitting in front of the mirror of Erised watching himself with his dead parents. You never knew about Harry Potter. He's a boy wizard whose parents died when he was a baby. The mirror of Erised is magic and shows you nothing more or less than your heart's desire. I know that if I looked in it I'd see you and me, grown up, maybe surrounded by children, our parents looking happily on. You have to be careful with the mirror, Harry is warned – you can go mad looking in it, yearning for what can't be. At some point, perhaps, I have to give more of my love to the living. I don't think you'd mind.

I will of course always wish you were here. I'll always miss the women that you would have loved and who would have become my friends, the children who would have been my nephews and nieces. I won't stop thinking that life is paler without you, that every single occasion would have been enlivened by you. I miss the arguments we might have had, the burdens we might have shared. I miss you as a confidant. I could tell you anything. You never sat in moral judgement, though I don't think I felt the pressure to be good until after your accident. When you knew me, I was just a girl, not a girl trying to be everything to her poorly brother and her shattered parents. I miss the way you would have told me to lighten up. If nature takes its course, I will miss you at the funerals of our parents, I will miss you at the births of any grandchildren I may have. If I steer clear of accidents, I'll miss you when I first start feeling tired, when I first find a lump, when I first get a diagnosis. Will I still be missing you at the end, I wonder? They say people return to their childhoods. Perhaps I won't have to miss you. Perhaps I'll spend my last moments jumping off the sofa with you, learning to fly.

Your ashes are still in Yorkshire. Shall I get you, my dear, would you like that? Shall I collect you from Mr Punton's and take you on a journey? I'm not a very good driver, but you don't have to worry about that. We could get the train. Go from Donny to King's Cross, over to Paddington and then down to Cornwall. I feel Cornwall is where you should be. I think you should mingle with the earth in the land where our parents met, under the ground where we once stood side by side.

I'll bring Matt to visit you and tell him about you, the other boy called Matthew, and how much I loved you. Maybe that's another act of love, for all of us.

You missed lots of things. You never had a mobile phone or used the Internet. I think about you when I realize that Matt eats things that I hardly knew existed until I went to university. I don't think you ever ate an avocado, an artichoke, aubergine or asparagus. And those are just the As.

But you didn't miss out on love. You were full of love, whether or not you wanted to doubt its existence. The last thing you said to our mother as you got out of the car at the Rainbow car park, as I was already on my way in to the noise and the music, was, 'I love you.'

You are so close to me now. I had lost you, buried under those eight years, but now I feel you. Sometimes I think you are walking down the street with me, telling me jokes. The other night, talking to a not very nice man at a party, I had the clearest picture of you tapping your forehead with your finger and looking me straight in the eye.

The thing I still don't know is whether or not you were at any level aware of your suffering. I hope you weren't.

Because if you weren't, if the essence of you didn't know what was happening during those eight years, then your first sixteen years were full of joy. It would be so wonderful to think that you never knew anything else.

If you did, at some level, know, if you did, even after those epileptic fits, somehow know what was happening to you, then I am glad that at least we brought you to your death when we did and that you aren't still there in a little room in Snaith Hall. It was, as Mum said, our last act of love for you.

That's enough, I hear you say. Fuck off, get over it. Stop banging on. I get it. Go on, go off and do something else.

I met a woman who believes in an afterlife. She told me that I should think of you as being free. She wasn't trying to convince me of anything, she just pointed out that whether there is an afterlife or not, you are at least liberated from your earthly prison. She also said that what helped her when she recently lost someone was trying to be grateful for the fifteen years they spent together rather than thinking only about the empty present.

I asked her who the person was that she had lost. I was wondering if it could be a child of fifteen or a close friend or lover she had known for fifteen years.

She looked a bit awkward. 'Well,' she said, 'it was my cat.'

And what I thought was lovely about this was that it showed me how I had healed. The old me, the angry me, the me who never managed to shed a tear for Polly, who envied people whose loved ones died a quick death, would have thought it ridiculous and obscene that someone could presume to think of you and a cat in the same way. This newer, softer, more reconciled version of me thought it was sweet. And a bit funny. And I thought you'd find it a bit funny too.

There's one more thing I want to tell you. It's a confession of sorts. All those Sunday afternoons growing up in Almond Tree Avenue, there were sweets after Sunday lunch. Do you remember? Always the same thing. A pack of six liquorice Catherine wheels with a pink or blue Allsort in the middle and a bar of pink-and-white-striped nougat. The parentally ordained rule to ensure good sharing was that whoever cut, the other one chose. The thing I want to tell you is that I had a technique where I cut your piece slightly smaller, but then stretched it to make it look bigger and trick you into choosing it, which you always did.

So I'm sorry about that. I'm sure you know that if I could go back in time there are many things I'd do differently, but I'd also not diddle you out of your fair share of nougat. You could have had all my nougat.

Love,

Your sister

AFTERWORD

It's a strange and beautiful thing to have a book out in the world. Despite working in books, I was unprepared for the emotional force of all those firsts: the first time I held a physical copy in my hand, my first reading, first review, first event, the first time I received a letter from a stranger, the first time I cuddled someone who had queued up to ask me to sign their book.

Perhaps because of the nature of my book, it feels like an ongoing and organic process. I've learned things about myself precisely because the questions I've been asked in interviews and at events, and the things people have told me about themselves, have helped to shape my thinking.

I've heard from a lot of bereaved siblings or from parents who have lost one child and tell me that my book helps them understand the experience of their surviving child. Because of all these conversations, I understand sibling loss now more clearly than I did before. It's a triple whammy of losing a person you love who has always been in your life – all my early memories have Matty in them; he was never not there – while you yourself are not fully formed, and the huge complexity of having to navigate parents who are now forever changed. I spoke about this with my friend Caroline, who remembers being upstairs on the night her sister died and hearing her parents sobbing in the kitchen below. 'I'd never heard either of them make noises like that,' she says, almost thirty years later.

I hear from people whose relatives are or have been in PVS and, again, my understanding has been broadened. It was only really when I was doing interviews for the book that I started to think about how terrible the situation must be when the person in PVS has children. What must it be like to grow up while your parent deteriorates? Or to be the surviving spouse who has to explain why Daddy isn't getting better, why Daddy isn't saying anything even though his eyes are open? That seems to me like a whole new bag of hell and why it is so important that this thorniest of subjects – we have not ethically, morally or legally caught up with our technical ability to prolong someone's life – is discussed.

I also hear from people who have witnessed some other kind of complicated and lengthy death. I can see that this is an increasing problem, one that will affect more and more of us in years to come.

People ask me a lot how involved my parents were before the book was published and how they feel about it all. I consulted with them at every stage and don't think I could have written it without their goodwill. They are both very proud of the response and they like coming to events and reading the letters I get sent.

My dad especially finds it very sad to remember those times, and as I was writing I often wondered whether it was right to put them through it all, but I had to cling to my conviction that it would be better for me, for them, and for little Matt to step into the silence we'd constructed around Matty and everything that happened to him.

A lot of people tell me they are familiar with the unspoken family pact of silence; that they are giving my book to someone else in the hope that it will encourage them to be able to speak about their own pain or loss.

I'm asked if the writing was therapeutic. Well, yes – I know I feel better than I did because I have succeeded in wrestling this complex subject out of me and on to the page. I've taken the tangled thoughts from my head and the sadness in every beat of my heart and put them into a book. The fact that the book is of use to other people feels like a miracle. I'm still a work in progress, though. Still struggling with the sadness, the never-ending zigzag of grief, and trying to do my best to live as though I deserve to be here.

The question that stumped me for ages was whether Matty would be proud of me. I couldn't wrap my head around all the conditionals – where he might be to be able to feel pride. And, as ever, the idea that anything that happened to me could be noteworthy given the magnitude of what happened to him seemed impossible. Then I thought about it some more and could imagine him saying, 'What's with all the crying?' and, 'For fuck's sake, will you get over it and do something else?'

And then, when the neurosurgeon Henry Marsh reviewed my book in the *New Statesman*, he very brilliantly contextualized it and I could imagine Matty being proud of that.

'Finally,' I hear him saying, 'finally, you've clocked that you should use your words to make sure some other poor fucker doesn't end up lying around for eight years like I did.'

Matty does pop up to tease me, swear at me and offer unsolicited career advice. ('What the fuck are you wasting time worrying about that for?') He's always swearing, always laughing and always encouraging me to lead a bigger, less fearful life. I have no idea whether he's in my head or in some way exists – and I'm not sure it matters. It's a gift to have even this slice of him, to know his speech patterns and his thoughts.

I was talking at an event in Bristol about how, possibly because I read too many novels, I often feel I'm stuck in the wrong narrative. In *Life After Life* by Kate Atkinson or *The Versions of Us* by Laura Barnett, for example, the narrative keeps showing us alternative universes where a significant event did or did not happen. I quite often feel that not only am I a character in a book, but also that there's a parallel universe out there – in life or on a shelf – where an undamaged version of me is living a joyous life.

Someone in that Bristol audience asked if I ever considered whether life could have worse, that perhaps I am in some way a stronger person because of Matty's accident.

'Oh, no,' I said. 'You see, in the other universe – the one that was taken away from me – my brother is a brain surgeon rather than being operated on by one; I've already written lots of books; our children are friends . . .'

I couldn't carry on. The thought of the little cousins my son might have had was too painful. Suddenly I was desolate.

I got lost on the way to catch my train home, was nearly hit by a bus and felt waves of panic sweeping through me. For a moment I thought I might collapse, but I got my breathing under control and found my way to the station one slow step at a time. On the train home – more trains, I'm always thinking on trains – I realized that most of what I have to do now is about committing to the storyline I'm in, rather than continuing to pine for the lost narrative.

And that's what I'm trying to do. It's a cruel world but there is beauty in it and perhaps the trick is in what we choose to pursue.

I've realized that the thing I most value is honest connection with other humans. I used to only dare look for that in books but now I see it in actual, real-life people. By writing my pain onto the page, by leaving space in this tale of one family's heartbreak for other people to identify and find common ground and solace, I've opened up a conversation. It's one I enjoy having.

Cathy Rentzenbrink
London, May 2016

Acknowledgements

The art of memoir-writing means that you leave a lot of people out and I want my first words here to be for everyone who loved Matty – I hope you think I've done a good job of putting him on the page. I'm also extremely grateful to all my friends, to those who mopped up tears in the time when I could talk about nothing else, and to more recent friends who suffered the disorienting experience of realizing there was rather a lot they didn't know about me. This reticence was no lack of love on my part, more a worry that if I started I wouldn't be able to stop. I'm truly grateful for every bit of kindness.

Work has often proved to be my salvation, and I'd like to give a wave to everyone who has ever stood with me behind a bar or a counter and to the many people who were both kind and interesting when I served them booze or books. I feel a special love for the customers at the Bell and Crown and for all my colleagues at Waterstones and Hatchards. I don't think it's much of an exaggeration to say that bookselling saved my life and I will always remember the joyous feeling that I had found my tribe. More recently, I'm indebted to Gail Rebuck for telling me to get some bigger dreams, to Julia Kingsford, Lisa Milton and Janine Giovanni for encouraging me to believe in myself, and to Claire de Boursac and Jo Dawson for being the lights of my Quick Reads life. Thanks to Nigel Roby, Philip Jones and Benedicte Page for making me so welcome at the *Bookseller*.

My husband Erwyn has always navigated my changes of mind with kindness and good humour, and was convinced long before I was that I would write a book, as were my dear friends John and Lizzie Waterhouse and Jo Dawson. I'm grateful to Tom Palmer for telling me to write it down and then making sure that I did it, with a wonderful blend of generosity, encouragement and bullying.

I still can't quite believe I'm allowed to use the word 'my' in relation to my agent Jo Unwin and my editor Francesca Main, who are pearls past price. I will be forever grateful for the skill and kindness with which they got this story out of me and onto the page. Heartfelt thanks to all at Picador and Pan Macmillan, especially Geoff Duffield, Anna Bond, Paul Baggaley, Camilla Elworthy, Justine Anweiler, Jon Mitchell, Claire Gatzen and Nuzha Nuseibeh, and to Juliet Van Oss for her copy-edit.

Finding the report on 'Prolonged disorders of consciousness' was transformative, as was getting to know Jenny Kitzinger and Julie Latchem. You can find out more about their work, including fascinating papers on media representations of coma, at www.cdoc.org.uk.

I'm not sure that the twenty-first-century woman does need a room of her own to write a book – I haven't got one – but really good childcare is essential so I'm grateful beyond measure to my wonderful child-minder Lynette Elske. Massive thanks also to my parents, to my aunt, Marion Bowyer, and my mother-in-law, Ada Rentzenbrink, for so regularly descending to look after Matt and liberate me from the tyranny of the laundry basket.

Thank you once more to my parents for travelling this hard road with me again. This book, and I, would not exist without their courage.

The last word goes to my little dude, Matthew Jan Rentzenbrink, who is both a joy and an inspiration and completely his own person. He is also a memory catalyst, and as I sing him the songs my dad sang to us, I feel surrounded by love.

Don't know what's comin' tomorrow
Maybe it's trouble and sorrow
But we'll travel the road, sharin' our load, side by side.